THE MULTINATIONAL MAN

THE MULTINATIONAL MAN

The Role of the Manager Abroad

by
THOMAS AITKEN

Consultant to
Business International S.A., Geneva
Centre d'Etudes Industrielles, Geneva

A HALSTED PRESS BOOK

JOHN WILEY & SONS
New York

Published in the USA
by Halsted Press, a Division
of John Wiley & Sons, Inc.
New York

© George Allen & Unwin Ltd 1973

Library of Congress Cataloging in Publication Data

Aitken, Thomas, 1910–
  The multinational man.

  "A Halsted Press book."
  Bibliography: p.
  1. International business enterprises.
2. Executives. I. Title.
HD69.17A47   658.1'8   73–10602
ISBN 0-407-01793-7

Printed in Great Britain in 11 point Times Roman by
The Aldine Press, Letchworth, Herts

Contents

Introduction

The title of a book is usually representative, symbolic or descriptive. In this case it is representative in that the book examines the role of one particular type of Multinational Man: the manager, director or managing director of a wholly owned foreign subsidiary of an international company. It does not include the Home Office executives in foreign departments or international divisions, or those domestic officers who give part of their time to a company's business abroad.

Also excluded are diplomats and officers of non-commercial international agencies, for theirs is another world. No discussions of multinational business, and this one is no exception, have dealt with the professions – legal, medical, architectural, dental, etc. – for their environment is the antithesis of the multinational world. These groups, basking in the reflected glory of specialized education and the badge of public prestige, are composed of primeval protectionists who openly and shamelessly erect national and provincial barriers against each other, and usually succeed in persuading their governments to legalize these barriers. A few individuals amongst them do achieve the intellectual growth to take an interest in international affairs, and periodically, the professions do exchange ideas internationally by means of specialized journals and the convocation of international conferences. These are exceptions to the custom of each national (and often provincial) professional group of barring its foreign or even local counterparts from practising within the confines of its preserve. The losers in this situation are the people of most countries.

Two more points require clarification. There are almost as many definitions of the multinational company as there are writers on the subject. Many, dissatisfied with the term, have proposed others such as international company, transnational company, cross-border business

9

or global enterprise. All are derivations of the concept of a company which has extended its business operations to other countries beyond its own. Rather than engage in a philological discussion, I have chosen to use these terms interchangeably, on the understanding that the global company has extended its business around the world without necessarily establishing a branch in every nation state.

Formerly accepted as components of the world's business structure, in the years since the Second World War the multinational companies have surged to the leadership of business everywhere. Those veteran firms whose international activities date from the early part of the century and before – mostly traders or harvesters of the raw materials of less-developed countries – have been joined by businesses of every description: manufacturers of consumer goods, financial services, and even hotel and restaurant chains. In every nation's list of major companies, those in international business now comprise the dominant sector.

It should not therefore be surprising that a spotlight of curiosity and interest has been turned on the men who represent the interests of these companies abroad. In their home countries they are often endowed with the halo of their predecessors, the adventurers who pried apart the barriers of distant lands to carve out fortunes for themselves, their monarchs and their countries. In the host nations that now receive these multinational men, this dramatic role is often tarnished with history's record of colonialism, as though the ghosts of former invaders had reappeared. In part this book seeks to clarify the question of who these men really are and what their role really is.

It does so with a minimum of references to joint ventures, because joint ventures vary so greatly in their composition, scope and duration that it is nearly impossible to define the role of the overseas manager of such an organization. Even the considerable body of written work about joint ventures has veered away from the topic of their management. Further studies of the subject may be expected, however, because although major companies have previously shown little interest in joint ventures, the tendency of many nation-states is to encourage or require them, and the Japanese multinationals are already taking the lead in exploiting their potential for profit.

Sources for the type of material used in this study rest primarily in the realms of experience, reading and association. While my exposure to the former has been extensive during twenty years spent abroad with the Interpublic Group of Companies, the latter has been most fruitful during my present activity as consultant to Business International and the Centre d'Etudes Industrielles. Although the ideas presented here are my own, acknowledgement is due to Mr Richard Conlon, formerly Managing Director of Business International S.A. (Europe), and since transferred to global responsibilities for the same firm in the United States. Mr Conlon's interest, ideas and the resources of his company's library have been invaluable.

No less stimulating has been the atmosphere of the Centre d'Etudes Industrielles, the school of advanced international management in Geneva. Fortunately, the CEI's library is administered by Dr Thérèse Seiler whose interest, and immediate appreciation of the subject, made her a constant and effective aide in organizing the information required.

Others, in past experience and present association, have contributed ideas for which I am grateful. First among them is my wife Barbara, a truly multinational woman, whose counsel, typing and copy editing helped make a book out of a headful of memories and observations plus a roomful of scattered documents.

Geneva, September 1, 1972

Chapter 1

The Multinational Man

In recent years much has been written about the international corporation, but little about the international man. History's revolving door spins all into its carousel, for even in this less dramatic aspect of human destiny a complete change has taken place. In former eras, epochs or centuries the international man was placed front of stage, with his company in the wings. He was the stuff from which the tales of Kipling, Conrad and Richard Harding Davis were drawn, and Macaulay found literary material in the international man's role as a displaced person. Finally, the romance of the man abroad filled the pages of many of Somerset Maugham's sagas. By then we knew the role of the international man: to be our own distant selves, to carry our dreams to the uttermost ends of the earth, there to find confirmation or to crumble under the challenge of the unknown. All this was endowed with the wonder of the readers, we who stayed at home, with our belief in revelation, our willingness to acknowledge the power of the unseen.

Technology changed us, and in many ways. One was to wipe out the reverie about discovery in far-off lands, another to erase bewilderment about the secrets of these lands. For mystery has vanished as the searchlight of technology has exposed life overseas, and distances have been reduced to the span of an airmail letter or a Telex message to the Orient. Suddenly the international man has become nothing more than the rest of us, grinding away at his daily work wherever he may be, while behind him, and looming over our lives, there has appeared the international company which employs him, the organization which the jargon of our times has named the multinational corporation.

The giant company of today is a multinational corporation and, while it has not found its way into the consciousness of our fiction writers, it has taken a leading role in our business literature. It has assumed this stance because it is big, larger than anything we have ever known in the economic world, and because it stands ready for a showdown of power with nation-states whose place in history is already being queried by political and sociological forecasters. Arnold Toynbee has reminded us that the nation-state as we know it is a relative new-comer on the world scene. It has spurted out of dying institutions or ancient empires like the European nations out of the Roman state, or has been implanted where tribal society existed before, as in America and Africa. Indeed, Toynbee contends that as the multinational com-pany becomes better able to satisfy society's future needs, it may well supersede the nation-state. But for all its power, despite its techno-logical accomplishments and the instruments which give such an organization instant knowledge and instant control of its far-flung activities, its destiny depends largely on the performance of its men abroad. At the nerve ends of the multinational corporation stands the international manager, the international executive. If both he and his company comprehend his role, and if he fulfils it well, the multi-national corporation may well achieve its nobler destiny as the swift communicator of knowledge and the effective investor of funds to alleviate the plights of underdeveloped economies and to develop an economic language common to all nations. The alternative destiny, which threatens the independence of nations, the purity of their cultures and the self-determination of their economic systems can, it has been predicted, lead to the death of multinational corporations, a death accelerated by the ineptness of their representatives at the far ends of the line.

These representatives, these international managers, are therefore called upon to fulfil a role less romantic and less subjective than their literary antecedents, but perhaps far more important to the world's wellbeing. The demand on the international manager as a human being is a many-dimensioned one. His predecessor's role was relatively simple. The eighteenth- and nineteenth-century company he rep-resented abroad operated to the benefit of its home government in return for which that government guaranteed its safety and usually its prosperity. The British, French and Dutch East India companies were prototypes which were succeeded by the oil, mining and rubber combines in a later century. All were able to rely on a regiment or a gunboat to secure their interests when the distant environment became querulous. The manager abroad knew that a single line of loyalty and authority led to headquarters and if necessary to the Foreign Office and the War Department. No interruption by host governments was permitted. Today if the residue of this history influences a board-room a company is heading for trouble, and when its man on the spot tends toward a Kiplingesque posture, he is immediately the wrong man for the job.

Operating today under the multiple demands and pressures of the home company's office management, home government policy, the attitude of his host government and the components of its society, the international manager begins by having to be a rather complex human being. One magazine has written:

'Ideally, it seems, he should have the stamina of an Olympic runner, the mental agility of an Einstein, the conversational skill of a professor of languages, the detachment of a judge, the tact of a diplomat, and the perseverance of an Egyptian pyramid builder. That's not all. If he is going to measure up to the demands of living and working in a foreign country he should also have a feeling for culture; his moral judgements should not be too rigid; he should be able to merge with the local environment with chameleon-like ease; and he should show no signs of prejudice.' [1]

This compendium of attributes is only one of many. Although most catalogues of an international manager's required virtues are less fanciful than the above, they do coincide on some points. One article states that the manager abroad must: (a) be adept at dealing with abstractions and variables, (b) have a flair for conceptual synthesis, (c) have a high degree of sensitivity and (d) a firm sense of values.

Another requires that managers be aware of themselves as culturally conditioned persons, be alert to the differences in perception between themselves and others, be aware of their own social needs and those of others and be willing to adapt and communicate. [2]

Endless lists have been drawn up citing the attributes required of a successful chief executive abroad or, rather, a successful overseas representative of a multinational company. Appropriately, most of them are more concerned with what kind of man the manager should

---

[1] 'What it Takes to Work Abroad', *International Management*, October 1970.
[2] *European Business*, Summer 1970.

be than with what kind of knowledge he should have. Of the human qualities recommended the most frequently named is sensitivity, sometimes called awareness, and often adaptability. Obviously this refers to a manager's need to acknowledge rather than ignore his environment. It doesn't mean he must 'do as the Romans do'. He might make a fool of himself at that game, unless he can also do it the *way* they do. In other words, adapt with grace rather than earnest clumsiness. Sensitivity might include discovering that Germans respond sympathetically to an effort to speak a few words of their language, even if badly, whereas the French scorn the foreigner who distorts their idiom.

The business environment is a vast area for a visitor to comprehend, particularly when it requires understanding a nation's social structure. Most natives do not understand the social structure of their own country which conditions them, but because it *does* condition them they live within it quite naturally unless they are young rebels, old eccentrics or the few thinkers who question rather than accept the premises offered them.

The trick for the international manager is to accept differences in life style and thereafter to seek the reasons for them. He will find in Latin America that businesses are run by autocrats, single strong personalities who in their fiefdoms parallel the man on horseback who is usually found in the country's history books to be that nation's historical hero. He will find that northern European businesses are mostly guided by boards, that French managers come from a few élite schools and that German managers come from technical academies. As Doina Thomas says: 'Most European nations have the style of management which the state of their economy demands.'[3] Accepting this statement requires an understanding of the culture and economic environment, but accepting it entirely can lead to pitfalls, especially when an economy is changing and its style of management is falling behind. This is undoubtedly occurring in Japan where only when the new generation of middle managers reach the top will they be able to bring their country's management concepts abreast of its social as well as economic needs.

Sensitivity, then, is accepted as an essential attribute for the international manager. Adaptability enables him to act in accordance with the learning that sensitivity gives him. But awareness is an attitude, and

[3] 'The Continental', *Management Today*, December 1969.

16

this can be assumed even when sensitivity comes in short supply. As one international management student at the Centre d'Etudes Industrielles (based in Geveva) remarked, the international manager should recognize other cultures as legitimate alternatives; he should be sceptical perhaps, but not cynical. And this will make it possible for him to make what may be the most important adjustment of all.

This realization concerns time and the arrangement of time that makes up a man's life. Thinking of his assignment abroad as transitory, limited to the period of his contract, can help an executive put up with the unpleasant aspects of his environment, but it will usually negate any efforts to understand or adjust to it. To consider oneself impermanent makes everything around one illusory and therefore valueless. There becomes little point in learning the language, so one seeks helpers who know it – and becomes dependent upon them. Because of this the daily newspapers, the radio, the television, the theatre, the conversation of people in a restaurant remain meaningless. One will not be in the same place more than a few years, so why invest in the comforts the local people enjoy – a Peruvian barbecue spit, a horse in Argentina, skis and lessons on the slopes in Switzerland, a Mercedes in Germany, a Cordon Bleu course in cooking for one's wife in France, subscriptions to some local clubs in Spain or even the books, records and furniture that make a home more comfortable? Why indeed invest time, money and energy in becoming part of the local scene when all this will some day disappear? Simply because it makes an executive a better manager and his family a happier group. It does more. It focuses a man's mind on the local scene. He need not forget London, or Cincinnati, or Toronto, but if that is where his mind is, energies that are required for a delicate and demanding job are diluted. Best that he return home as soon as possible because abroad he is losing the use of his subconscious mind, the area that never stops working or dreaming and often unexpectedly reveals solutions to problems.

There are, however, other kinds of managers of international companies. There are the nationals hired on the spot or taken on as second men and trained for managership. There is the growing class of international 'professionals' whose nationality is a minor factor and who are transferred from country to country in accordance with their employers' expediency. Where does their need for sensitivity lie, if there is one? In what direction does their awareness lead them? And to what do they

17

have to adapt? If they are moved to a country other than their own, their problems are much the same as those of men sent out from the company's home office – except that they do not identify the home office with home. These are truly the professionals of the trade, a small but growing élite in the multinational world. In their case the human attributes we have been discussing become, and are, professional qualifications.

The national who accepts representation of a multinational company in his own country is perhaps best served by overlooking his possibly equivocal position. We asked one if the same sensitivity was required of him as it would be of a man from headquarters sent to his country:

'Sensitivity? Sensitivity to what?'

'Not to your country, of course. It's yours. But perhaps to the fact that you are serving a company whose objectives may not parallel those of your government.'

'But that happens with our own national companies. Why should I be so concerned about that?'

Our taxi stopped for a traffic light at this point, allowing for a moment of reflection.

'But let us suppose that your employer's policies', we persisted, 'were contrary to your own government's objectives. Where would your loyalties tend?'

'I do my job in that case, understanding, of course, that there is no question of national security involved. After all, a government's policies can change with the next election. We usually hope they will.'

'So if you have no need to be unusually acute about the atmosphere surrounding you because it is yours anyway – perhaps you have to tune your antennae when they turn to your company's home office because that is foreign territory.'

'Ah, now I understand you. Of course.'

'This is a question of communications?'

'But of course. Why didn't you ask me that before?'

The question of communications deserves comment in another chapter, but the national manager facing that problem may have to call on the same personal reserves in dealing with his company's home office as the home office man abroad. For the manager hired or trained

18

abroad, company headquarters are the exotic environment. They represent concepts of business operations different from those in his native country. Although they usually seek some accommodation between their own philosophy and those prevailing overseas, headquarters do not go so far as to relinquish the home office viewpoint, and the national manager abroad must learn to represent it even when it jars against the policies and mores of his homeland. His income is now dependent on a foreign source and his career is committed to a power outside his own country. This is *his* problem of awareness to a strange environment, an environment physically distant but in his work always present. Directives from headquarters, the visits of executives and supervisors from the home office are constant reminders that there is a continuing call on his loyalties from beyond his country's borders.

Whereas this pressure on the loyalties of the national manager abroad – and to some degree on that of the headquarters representative who has stayed overseas for some years – was once only important in the underdeveloped countries which have long seen the multinational company as a threat to their sovereignty, it may now exist in the most advanced of nations, for the multinational firm has expanded its power to such an extent that all nations view it as a challenge to their sovereignty.

This has not aroused unreserved hostility toward the multinational company. There is recognition even in Servan-Schreiber's plea for an adequate European defence against the American incursion that the multinational firm brings benefits which nations cannot ignore. Most nations still try to attract multinational business, although increasingly on a selective basis. They accept the multinationals' capital and their ability to contribute to capital formation within the country. They know that the multinational organization is a tremendously effective transmitter of technology and management, that it can aid in the development of depressed areas of a country, that it can create new sources of exports to help a nation's balance of payments. In fact the power to make beneficial contributions is so great on the part of the multinational firm that its ability to withhold its participation in a nation's economy may be a threat to that nation's growth. And it may keep its distance if one nation's tax policies are less attractive than another's, or if its political environment is less stable or less friendly, or if its currency is less dependable. By staying out, the multinational firm affects a nation's growth. By entering, it may operate according to its own and not to its host country's economic plan, for its action in one country is only a part of its multinational policy.

The international manager in most cases has learnt to live with the open or disguised discord of his company with the nation where he is employed. But new areas of responsibility are looming for the multinational company as its significance in world affairs increases and as its weight on society is increasingly discernible. These responsibilities place new strains on the international manager as a human being, bringing his conscience and company policy to further points of divergence. The company's influence on the values of currencies, its policies toward labour and the employment of minorities, its effects on pricing and wage levels and, most notably, its influence on the physical environment are being called to account. Where the international manager stands in the midst of this arena, as when American companies and others move vast funds against a national currency, or when an American company attempts to reconcile its employment policies in South Africa with the anti-apartheid demands of the American public, or a German company is refused entrance to an American state because of its threat to the environment while it continues to pollute its own district in Germany – when these situations occur, the international manager is, to borrow the term and change its meaning, the man on the spot. He will be more so as these pressures increase.

In these circumstances a new dimension is added to the qualities required of international management working away from the home office. It shares this social concern with the domestic manager who, in the words of the *Harvard Business Review*,

'. . . is almost sure to be a troubled man . . . But this does not necessarily mean that the critically motivated executive can do nothing. In fact, if he does nothing, he may so bleach his conception of himself as a man of conviction as to reduce his personal force and value to the company. His situation calls for sagacity as well as courage. Whatever ideas he advocates to express his sense of social responsibility must be shaped to the company's interest.

'Asking management flatly to place social values ahead of profits would be foolhardy, but if he can demonstrate that, on the basis of long-range profitability, the concept of corporate efficiency needs to be broadened to include social values, he may be able to make his point without injury – indeed with benefit – to his status in the company . . .

'It may be that the future of our enterprise system will depend on the emergence of a sufficient number of men of this breed who believe that in order to save itself business will be impelled to help save the society.'[4]

[4] *Harvard Business Review*, July–August 1970.

Chapter 2

The Small Multinationals

Evaluations of managerial talent tend to follow the conventions used for categorizing university graduates. One of them assumes that the bigger and more prestigious the university, the bigger and more promising the man. This has been an easy shortcut for personnel managers, minimizing the time they must allot to the analysis of potential employees. It has also seeped into the thinking of management and of executives concerned with the search for managerial talent.

The man from Unilever will more quickly be granted consideration for an important post in marketing than a recent partner in Blimey's Fish 'n Chips. The extension of this credo – based on some justifiable assumption – to international thinking tends unduly to shrink the pool of available managerial talent. It can, and probably should, be broadened by an appreciation of the qualities required to manage a small enterprise when it goes abroad.

The international business scene has been described in broad strokes and headline type because it has been the most impressive area of business growth since the Second World War. And the leaders of the Big Parade have been companies already swollen with success in their own countries (some being early veterans in the international field). Their expansion has led Professor Howard Perlmutter of the Wharton School to predict that by 1985 two to three hundred firms will conduct most of the world's business. This thesis has been challenged, and Professor Perlmutter has qualified his forecast with the admission that there will be room in the sea for small fish as well. Statisticians have told us that in 1968 the assets of multinational enterprises totalled $94 billion and that their foreign sales exceed the gross national product (GNP) of all countries except the U.S. and the U.S.S.R. About 55 per cent of these assets are owned by American companies. The foreign output of such companies has been expanding at the rate of 10 per cent, or twice the rate of world GNP, and 40 per cent faster than world exports.

Although British, Swiss, Dutch and other national firms have been in the vanguard of this prosperous advance, the big figures indicate the presence of American corporations. Of the 500 largest American firms, those whose foreign sales and/or assets represented 25 per cent or more of their total business in 1967 grew by 64 per cent over the preceding five years. Companies doing less than 25 per cent of their business abroad expanded by 53 per cent over the same period.

As incisive, if perhaps less gargantuan, are figures cited by Stig Ramel in an address to the Swedish Marketing Association in October 1970. He said:

'Let me express Sweden's international dependence in concrete figures: 40–45 per cent of our industrial production is sold abroad. Swedish capital invested abroad rose more than 80 per cent between 1960 and 1965, and statistics on permits granted indicate a trebling since then.

'Swedish factories overseas had a 1965 turnover equal to 2/5 of total Swedish exports. Twenty-one groups accounted for most of the Swedish companies abroad and these groups' parent companies in Sweden accounted for 25 per cent of Swedish exports.'

Mr Ramel had some thoughts about the growth of Swedish companies abroad that differed in more than nuance from the conventional explanations of cross-border expansion:

'Formerly they were run primarily to circumvent tariffs and other trade obstacles, to eliminate transport costs and to make use of local sources of raw materials. Trade liberalization and the transport revolution have not, however, brought about a slower rate of establishing subsidiaries abroad. On the contrary, the rate has increased, and there is reason for believing that this trend of development will become even more marked during the seventies. The principal motive force behind this trend is more and more proximity to the consumer, the need to let production be suited to the market and the possibilities of widening areas of contact with technical and economic events all over the world. Do not overlook the fact that a subsidiary overseas is not only a manufacturing, sales and service station but also a listening post and a source of ideas for the whole group.'

Mr Ramel seemed to reveal further original thinking when he went on to say:

'People often consider there is a conflict of interests between large and small companies. Actually, there is in my opinion a situation in which fruitful interaction can take place. Innovation companies are often launched by engineers and technical staff from the major companies, led by people who want to manage the development of their ideas by themselves. The prerequisites are there for the small companies to engage in fruitful collaboration with the big cross-national companies, not only traditionally as sub-contractors but also as suppliers and mediators of new technology . . . The vision of a future world dominated by a few mammoth companies controlled far above ordinary men's heads is therefore in my opinion too static and stereotyped.'

Mr Ramel's view probably also takes into account the fact that anywhere one may look there are more small companies than large ones and that no matter how many are absorbed by the giants other energetic little fighters will take their places. Perlmutter concedes that the bantam-weight companies will survive because of their agility and their special abilities to supply products of high technological worth to limited markets, and to offer technically specialized services.

Some, not all, of the benefits that giant firms offer host countries are found in the repertoire of small companies. They cannot bring impressive infusions of capital or vast employment opportunities; nor can they contribute with massive exports to boost the nation's balance of payments. But they can and do bring with them a high degree of technological skill and because they have small reserves of disposable managerial talent in their own home offices they are prepared, even anxious, to employ local nationals abroad for top managerial jobs.

Small companies able to go abroad are equipped with specialized skills that serve the local community and can be sub-contracted to the large local firms as well as to the multinational firms in the area. Their survival depends on service, and those who can cross national borders have a high measure of service to offer, in products or talent, or else they must stay within their home markets.

Although the benefits they provide to a national economy are less sumptuous than those of the giant multinationals, smaller companies do not convey the threats to national sovereignty which are classically associated with large multinational corporations. They cannot dislocate employment or wage patterns. They cannot evade tax obligations with transfer pricing nor threaten the currency value with massive shifts of funds, nor can they weigh heavily against the national economic plan in following a global plan of their own. There is also little possibility that they may be disguised instruments of their home government's foreign policy.

To survive they must be agile, serviceable and able to purvey the goods or services needed wherever they settle abroad.

In an economic system where survival often depends on sheer power on one side or on technological skill or creative service on the other, the specialized small company with wit and the ability to satisfy consumer needs will find a place, and need not restrict its activity to one country.

There is, for example, a company based in Monaco (for fiscal reasons) which provides and supervises franchises for while-you-wait shoe repairs in department store booths throughout Europe. The company is highly successful; its franchises number well over one thousand. There is no revolutionary quality about the machinery which it provides to its licensees, but it is better than that which shoe repair shops have had before, and there are ways of using it that give a customer fast, satisfactory and reasonably priced service. But the company is not necessarily primitive because its product is simple. Its executives are to be seen at most business symposia in Europe and it subscribes to the same advanced information services whose advisory publications are read by senior executives of the major multinational companies.

A counterpart on perhaps a more glamorous level is the Computer Machinery Corporation of Los Angeles, California, which in 1969 could claim only $2 million in capital and 75 employees. A year later, with a subsidiary in England and another in France, its capital had risen to $6 million and its payroll had swollen to 475. Its product is a replacement for key punches, serving the market for data entry systems and input equipment. Its adventure abroad was reported in an article published by the *Harvard Business Review*[1] where the advantages of the small cross-border company were accented in the statement that:

---

[1] *Harvard Business Review*, September–October 1970.

'A small U.S. company operating in Europe has some advantages over the larger one. Because the little fellow has far less impact on the host country, he is more likely to be left alone by the government than is the giant whose every move generates economic repercussions.

'Understandably, labour unions too pay little attention to the small company, probably viewing it as not worth the effort.'[2]

A second characteristic of the small company abroad, as exemplified by the Computer Machinery Corporation, is that it carries a message about the manager of such a firm, an inadvertent signal to the large companies as to where the talent pool may be.

'To speed the start-up process,' says CMC, 'we patterned the English subsidiary after our parent company. For motivational and political reasons, however, we are insisting that the English operation be as independent as possible in pursuing its objectives. We have not merely hoisted a Union Jack over a group of Americans, as many companies do. We have set certain guidelines and goals and turned the subsidiary's management loose.

'We are convinced that the best way to run our overseas – and domestic – operations is to select high-quality people, motivate them and let them run their own show.'

Third among the attributes of small international companies which affect the character and role of the manager abroad is the tendency to hire local nationals wherever possible, and for the small companies it seems to be possible. CMC's policy is

'. . . part of a plan to maintain a low profile overseas . . . This is true not only in the case of workers and technical personnel, but also managers – including the head of the operation. There are a number of obvious – and not so obvious – reasons why this is good practice.

'If the managers we hire are good business men they will be far more effective in their familiar environments than most transplanted Americans could be for some time – maybe ever. The subtle nuances of doing business that often trip up Americans are second nature to nationals.

'Hiring nationals is the best way to overcome the language problem . . .

[2] *Ibid.*

'You may avoid sending one or more of your key managerial or technical persons overseas permanently. Thus you can prevent weakening the parent company – especially if it is a smaller one . . .

'Having nationals in management positions is very helpful, if not downright essential, in the government dealings that inevitably are a major element of doing business overseas . . .'

Most of the small enterprises extending their operations across national borders lack none of the sophistication of their bigger brothers. Many are launched, as Stig Ramel has said, by men who have left major companies and who were impelled by the desire to fulfil their own ideas in their own manner. But not all such companies are new-comers on the business scene, although their international initiatives may be recent.

One such company is the Yarway Corporation, headed by D. Yarnall Jr. Yarway has a history which reaches as far back as the two world wars. It was founded in 1908 in Blue Bell, Pennsylvania, U.S.A., by Mr Yarnall's father and Bernard G. Waring. The Yarnall Waring Company, now the Yarway Corporation, has never strayed far from its original purpose, to make and sell the best possible valves, gauges, pumps, traps, power plant products and steam specialities for in-dustrial use.

Yarway, like many smaller companies, is not just a face in the crowd, lost among massive multinational corporations or large corporations on its home ground. The stamp of an individual defines its leadership which is not obliterated by thousands of stockholders or by faceless financial backers. Founded in the heart of Quaker Pennsylvania, Yarway is dedicated to excellence in its product, and it is also devoted to Quaker principles. It is a company that has deemed it proper to publish a booklet entitled *Basic Policies* whose preamble states that:

'Yarway Corporation recognizes the mutual opportunities that characterize its relationships with its customers, employees, stock-holders, suppliers and surrounding communities. This recognition leads the Board of Directors and Management to believe that it is desirable to publish the company's Basic Policies.'

Prominent among these policies is the statement that:

'The company should be operated to enrich the lives of all people

27

affected by it. Every effort should be made to respect the dignity and worth of all persons. Distinctions will not be made between people because of race, religion or natural origin.'

Complementing that concept is the declaration that:

'The company should grow according to plan. Growth should be in human relationships, creativeness, capacity and productiveness, as well as in sales volume and profitability . . . The rate of growth should be no faster than can be staffed by well qualified, properly oriented employees.'

Lest there be any illusion that good works in Yarway mean softness in business capability, the Yarway annual report clearly spells out the company's objectives (in 1970) and states its comparable achievements. Total sales volume should increase at an average rate of 12 per cent a year; the 1970 record was 13 per cent. Net profit should average at least 7 per cent of sales and 12 per cent of net worth; the accomplishment was 5 per cent of sales and 10·7 per cent of net worth – short of the target but 64 per cent ahead of the previous year's mark. In product development, the declared target is: 'One truly new product line per year, plus additions, extensions and improvements to present product lines.' The goal was reached.

Perhaps the remarkable accomplishment of Yarway is its success in combining an appreciation of human values with its recognition of the most advanced principles of management. Its label for this development is, not surprisingly, 'teambuilding'. Its annual report tells us:

'. . . that we usually obtain best results by bringing together the people who are most concerned about a problem and encouraging them to work together to arrive at the best solution – a process that is often accompanied by an increasing sense of common purpose and mutual trust . . . through the utilization of Task Groups, each formed for a specific purpose and then disbanded when the objective is accomplished.'

Finally we come to Yarway's interest in international activities. The report states that:

'Our efforts to serve society and earn a good profit have led us to extend Yarway's business around the world. The Canadian and British subsidiaries are thriving. Yarway N.V. in Europe is making steady progress along the road to profitability and our export business is growing steadily. In Japan we are well represented by an excellent agent and manufacturing licensee and we are currently engaged in discussions with them about our future in the Far East.'

Yarway's net sales in 1970 were $16,108,000 and its personnel totalled 500 men and women. Robert Yarnall Jr, while on his sabbatical from the Presidency, is Chairman of the Education Committee of the Young Presidents' Association of the United States.

Yarway is not a phenomenon among small companies, neither is the Computer Machinery Corporation, nor are our friends in Monaco. Each has the time for humanity, but none is overtaken by naïvety. They share, each in its own way, the stamp of individuality, but none disdains the advances of scientific management. Important in the trajectory which they have outlined for themselves is an awareness that in going abroad they are entering the territory of the stranger, but that by bringing a service and stepping softly they have found an open door.

Also common to these and other small companies is the inclination toward taking on local nationals as their managers abroad. Yarway employs no Americans abroad, CMC's men abroad are men of the host country and the Monaco company's licensees are local small business men.

These small companies, a large and ever growing band spreading among nations their expertise, their technology and their services, are creating on the home soil of their host nations a pool of managerial talent. Not able to afford the complex control systems of the giants, they must leave the day-to-day supervision of their field operations to trusted local lieutenants, men who learn the techniques of their business and who absorb the spirit of adaptive entrepreneurship that makes them go. Free of the ponderous bureaucracy of big business, but associated with the technical advantages of modern management, the overseas representatives of such companies have every opportunity to move ahead of their counterparts and to out-manœuvre the entangled managers sent abroad by large corporations. The odds are that the massive multinationals will eventually search among this expanding group of managers for the men to head their own operations abroad.

And the probability is that few such managers will be enticed to exchange the human relationships, the flexibility and the pure fun of doing business in a small but bustling organization for whatever enticements the major companies can offer.

Senior executives of several hundred European companies who met in Davos, Switzerland, during the 1972 European Management Forum, studied the challenges to survival of moderate-sized firms and considered some specific cases reported by Business International in one of its briefing papers. Excerpts from that paper are worth further study and are presented here.

The small companies successful in the international arena have often the following features in common:

High specialization. They specialize in one or a few top-quality products, often with a high unit-value. Thus the electronic machine produced by Gleason Works of the United States may cost up to $1 million apiece while Kudelski of Switzerland sells some models of its Nagra recorder at around $1,500. Often, too, these firms' customers are few and loyal, and are given personal service.

Technological lead over competitors. To keep abreast of competition, the successful small firm normally spends a high percentage of its turnover on research and development, e.g. 12 per cent to 15 per cent in the case of Digitron of Switzerland. Its workforce often contains an unusually high ratio of engineers and laboratory personnel, e.g. 30 engineers out of a total payroll of 125 in the case of Digitron.

Jealous attachment to financial independence. The capital of these firms is generally concentrated in a few hands or at least tightly controlled by a friendly group of large shareholders (to avoid a surprise takeover, shares are often not quoted and not registered). Reliance on self-financing is widespread and often profits are reinvested for future growth.

Lean managerial structures. In most firms the managerial team is compact, with key decisions taken by one man or a very small board. Purely administrative chores are kept to a minimum. Conversely, to develop loyalty and dedication among their personnel, successful small

firms often make a point of nurturing a collegial or participitive atmosphere.

Manufacturing autonomy. To avoid suppliers' delays or inadequate performances, even very small firms tend to manufacture as many components as possible for incorporation into the final product.

Aggressive marketing techniques. For an important order, the chief
executive officer or owner of the firm often follows the client directly,
giving him the feeling that his needs receive the closest attention at the
very top. Some specific cases illustrate the above points.

Naarden – The Dutch Perfumer

A modest chemical manufacturer before the Second World War,
Naarden of the Netherlands has developed into an international company established in twenty-two countries and supplying 200 different
fields of industry, and is now one of the world's largest and most
versatile producers of basic perfumes, essences and flavourings.

Founded in 1905 as a glycerine distiller, Naarden is now active in
major product categories ranging from perfume compounds used by
French perfumers to odoriferants and flavourings, and from bulk
chemicals to anti-oxydants.

Naarden follows a policy of direct control by headquarters personnel
over its overseas distribution system. Not a single Naarden product is
marketed through an independent distributor, because the company feels
that outsiders could not give the technical assistance and advice required
by its customers. Foreign countries where there is no local Naarden
plant are covered by about 100 company agents marshalled in different
regional areas, by sales supervisors, by travelling salesmen from Holland,
or by small local sales offices combined with mixed workshops.

Naarden's widespread foreign operations resulted in the setting up of
a special international management organization. At the Dutch headquarters an executive team reporting to the general managing director
centralizes control of production, sales, finance and research and development. Each team manager has his opposite number in every
foreign subsidiary, with the local man having full responsibility for
day-to-day management. The sales division functions on an area
and product basis, subdivided into bulk chemicals and tailor-made

products. A flying squad of technical, financial and sales experts deals with emergency problems at the top.

Moulinex – A Champion of Household Gadgets
One firm that has derived maximum benefits from the emergence of the European mass market is Société Moulinex of France. Created in 1956, Moulinex immediately produced a coffee grinder that revolutionized French coffee making. At $4 it found that the price was not only unbeatable in France but also abroad. In Germany, even with the then existing customs duties, Moulinex grinders sold at less than half the cheapest local brand on the market. Thanks largely to its aggressive pricing policy in the sixties, Moulinex was able to frustrate the efforts of a larger U.S. competitor, Scovill, to establish a manufacturing base in France.

Recognizing the tremendous demand potential for small domestic appliances, Moulinex lost no time in introducing complementary products onto the market. By 1960 the company was already producing electric mixers, choppers and other kitchen appliances in addition to its grinders. It was in that year that Moulinex decided to enter the hairdryer market, and it sold about ten times the previous domestic demand in its first year of production (in 1959, 75,000 dryers were sold in France; in 1960, 852,000 were sold – virtually all were Moulinex).

Moulinex' rapid growth has been the fruit of its imaginative marketing methods and constant diversification of its product lines – sales, which stood at $20 million four years after the firm was founded, soared to over $50 million last year.

There are probably three main factors in the success of the company's operations – the expanded market created by the EEC, integrated mass production and a strict control over distributors' operations.

The Common Market, with a population of 170 million,[3] provides an enormous opportunity for growth in itself; however, Moulinex sees it as a base for building a strong export market. The company exports its products in 112 countries around the world, and for the future looks enviously at the 200 million U.S. market.

Oće-Van der Grinten – Rapid International Expansion
Another Dutch firm that is growing fast by crashing into new terri-

[3] Before the Nine.

tories while managing to preserve its identity is Océ-van der Grinten of Venlo.

Its turnover rose by 42 per cent in 1970 to $85·8 million, just over ten times that of 1961. Its goal is 5 per cent of the world copying market by 1975.

Its specialized output is based largely on various forms of printing reproduction, including carbonless copy paper for computers, equipment for audio-visual use and similar material. About 80 per cent of its turnover has come from paper processing and the remainder from copying machines, but the latter proportion is now growing. About 90 per cent of its output is sold in Europe, 3 per cent in Africa, 3 per cent in Australia and 1 per cent in Asia.

The four main pillars of Océ's policy are: continuous specialized research (which occupies 7 per cent of its staff), establishment of new overseas subsidiaries, international expansion by takeovers and the acquisition of exclusive rights. The first foreign subsidiary was established in Germany in 1958, and since then Océ has set up others, mostly fully owned, in Austria, Sweden, Denmark, Norway, England, Luxembourg, France (two), Italy, Belgium, South Africa, Australia and the U.S.

A big step forward was taken in July 1970 when Océ decided to enter the U.S. market and challenge the very large companies established there. It first acquired its Pittsburg licence (for its diazo papers), and B. K. Elliott Co., which was a supplier of dyeline products and electrostatic copiers, and has since been rechristened Océ-Elliott.

In January 1971 Océ-Elliott acquired a 65 per cent interest in ICP of Chicago, a producer of electrostatic copying equipment, which is now part of Océ's European line.

Gleason Works – Technology plus Marketing
Specialization and technological sophistication have been the keys to success in the international arena for Gleason Works of the U.S. Engaged in international trade for over eighty years, the company has literally geared its growth to the automotive industry, which provided over 70 per cent of its turnover ($70 million in 1970). But Gleason does not feel confined by the automotive market; it already has contracts from the helicopter, turbine jet and fast-growing pleasure-boat industries.

33

Until recently Gleason relied mainly on domestic production to service the world market, but this is changing. The company already has a plant in England that produces cutters for the European market and Japan, and recently decided to build a new $10 million plant in Belgium that will produce a range of smaller machines for the growing European small-car market. Originally it was planned to build the plant in the New York area . . . This plant when completed may well become an excellent base for supplying East European orders. The company has already been awarded a $22·5 million order for equipment by the U.S.S.R. and a $1 million order from the Fiat licensee in Yugoslavia. In addition Gleason is negotiating a contract worth some $10 million for the Kama River truck project in the U.S.S.R.

It was the Gleason Works which developed a unique design principle for gears (in a car's differential) that is in use around the world today . . . The company puts great emphasis on keeping ahead technologically and about 5 per cent of total corporate expenditure is spent on research and development.

Capital requirements for expansion meant that in 1958 the company ceased to be 100 per cent family owned, and although 58 per cent of the shares are now in the hands of the public, the company sees no danger of being taken over.

Kudelski – A Leading Specialist

Kudelski of Cheseaux, Switzerland, the undisputed leader in the field of professional recorders, is the brainchild of a Polish-born inventor, Mr Stefan Kudelski, who still owns 100 per cent of the company. As an electronics-oriented youth, Mr Kudelski discovered the portable magnetic tape recorder. He made himself one at home in his spare time, 'to see how the thing worked'. Professional radio people who came into contact with it assured Mr Kudelski he had a better product on his hands than anything else then made. Kudelski launched into production.

For quite a few years, the operation was largely based on artisan labour, and turnover in 1968 – five years after the foundation of the company – was only Sfr434,000, for a production of 240 recorders, with a total payroll of twenty-four.

Last year sales had reached $2·5 million, based solely on the Nagra recorder, but by 1973 the firm plans to be producing five different products. Distribution is simple (low volume: high unit-price); Kudelski has three sales companies (U.S., France, U.K.) which he has set up on a 50–50 basis with local partners and some twenty agents in major cities. The company currently has a payroll of 300.

Mr Kudelski attributes the success of his firm to:

High specialization. This gives it a *de facto* technological advance. Development is a constant activity of the firm, which spends 7 per cent of its turnover on research and development.

Systematic short-circuiting of intermediaries. This occurs not only at the selling end, but also at the purchasing level (its sales companies in the U.S., France and the U.K. double as purchasing companies for Mr Kudelski).

Technical autonomy. Kudelski manufactures all but the electronics components mentioned above. This avoids suppliers' delays and cuts the time from the moment the product is put on stream to the point when it is finally marketable.

Simple decision-making structure. Mr Kudelski takes important decisions, in the last resort. For psychological reasons he does strive, however, to nurture a collegial atmosphere.

Chapter 3

Strategist and Planner

On an autumn afternoon in Geneva, a group of forty-two young men from seventeen different countries – average age thirty-three – were assembled to analyse the situation of an American company on the verge of investing in a manufacturing facility in Singapore. The day was grey and dull, provoking no temptation to gaze through the picture windows of the classroom (they were in a management education school) in dreamy contemplation of the grassy slopes leading to the trees screening the River Arve.

Before them stood a young Harvard-trained professor, keen, experienced in living abroad (Tunisia, Venezuela, now Europe) and adept at leading a group analysis such as this towards the heart of a business problem.

The case was not a complex one. An American car radio manufacturer was considering the establishment of a factory in Singapore to fabricate and supply radios and subassemblies for its home base in Detroit. Customers of the home factory were the major car manufacturers in the United States. Singapore, with its supply of cheap labour and its incentives for foreign investors – low taxes, cheap land and free import of raw materials – could offer a source for the home factory which might well give it a cost advantage over competitors in the United States.

There were unresolved questions, however. The political climate in Singapore might change. A cash investment would have to be made. Profits for the Singapore factory would have to be limited in order to hold taxes to a level where a savings in production costs abroad would not be nullified. And there were attractive incentives in the possibility of locating the venture in other sites such as Taiwan, Hong Kong or Seoul.

Another factor to be taken into account was the understanding that

36

this venture abroad would have only one customer, the home factory in Detroit. But the company was not a novice in the international field; it had done well with similar direct investments in Mexico, Australia and with a minority position in a Japanese company.

The Geneva students – called participants by management development schools – engaged in a lively discussion of the case, considering risks, cash flow and alternatives. One young executive stated that he would not have accepted the job of manager in Singapore because the parent company planned for tax reasons to impose a ceiling on the profits of the Singapore subsidiary, and he would feel that his capacity and the results of his efforts would be unfairly judged under such a constraint. Those who had read about the global philosophy of international companies, and how subsidiaries were expected to contribute to total rather than local goals, attempted to correct this recalcitrant's viewpoint, but he stubbornly insisted that a company forgets its global view when it is judging the individual performances of its managers abroad, and he would not submit to a situation that condemned him in advance to a limited achievement. The discussion continued as to whether the company should install a subsidiary in Singapore.

After the afternoon coffee break the group returned to its classroom to read a short memorandum distributed by the professor, who enjoyed the superior position of having prior knowledge. The memorandum described what had finally occurred. The company had indeed made the investment in Singapore. It had found an alert Malaysian manager, Mr Koo Kim, with former experience in electronics in Japan, and the local plant had been expeditiously built and put into operation with not more than a few months' delay beyond the target date.

The first year's operations met all objectives. In the second year the home company began to accumulate a growing inventory because car production in the United States was diminishing. Hence the need for sources from Singapore decreased. This unfortunate state of affairs persisted and Singapore was ordered to reduce its output just at the stage when it was reaching its maximum capacity. The Malaysian manager protested that a cutback would leave the plant with idle workers. He suggested that he seek other customers for his products. He felt confident that he could find buyers. The home company, aware that his other customers might be competitors of their major, and treasured, clients, declined his suggestion and requested that he cut payroll costs by dismissing factory personnel immediately.

Mr Kim replied that this would be suicidal in Singapore where employers might pay low wages but were not allowed to fire workers at will. The government had views on such questions, democratically imposed, and its attitude could be, indeed would be, particularly firm in the instance of an enterprise from abroad. He again offered to find other buyers for the plant's products.

Mr Kim's arguments fell flat in Detroit. The parent company was losing orders. Moreover its own workers, through their union leaders, were warning the company that if there were any layoffs in Detroit because of cheaper labour being used abroad there would be very serious trouble at the home office.

Again the cables told Mr Kim to dismiss his Malaysian and Chinese workers. The jobs of the Americans in Detroit had to be saved.

Mr Kim resigned. The Singapore plant was closed. The investment was written off. What went wrong? Obviously, as a case study, the question that had not been asked in the first place was, what assurance was there that the home factory, the only customer of the Singapore plant, could increase its sales to absorb the additional materials that Singapore would provide?

But in Mr Kim's personal case he had failed to seek answers to other important questions. What kind of company am I going to work for? To whom in the company will I really be reporting? There was an international department in this company, and Mr Kim had assumed that its head was his chief. However, his only customer was the home factory which he would supply with radios and subassemblies and the chief of this plant reported to the president of the company. When the crisis came the head of the international division had no authority over company policy, and the head of the Detroit plant had no concern about Mr Kim and all his far-off compatriots. This was a company with an ineffectual international division which had put an overseas manager into a position of dependence on a product line executive whose concerns were primarily domestic.

What made this a good case for aspiring international managers to study was its many implications. Here was a company which had committed all, or nearly all, the sins ascribed to international companies. Only its modest size and its failure may have prevented it from committing more. It had entered a friendly host country with a minimum investment; much of its capital had been raised with help from the host government. Its business was not complementary to the host country's broad economic plan. It had no plan for reinvestment of profits in the host country. It hired and fired with no concern for local labour policies. And its goal was purely a commitment to the home company's priorities.

None of these points were emphasized in the deliberations of the group studying the case. It was led to concentrate on what was good for the company rather than how it might contribute to the concept of world citizenship for companies who seek the privileges of world citizens. Forgotten entirely was the destruction of a rare commodity, perhaps the most scarce in cross-border business: a good manager, Mr Kim.

Better informed, Mr Kim might have avoided linking his career with catastrophe. He might have undergone the academic exercise of classifying the company in order to understand his role. It would not have been a simple task and his sources would not have been definitive, but they would have been indicative enough to allow scope for his own judgement. One type of definition could have been found in a book like *The Strategy of Multinational Enterprise* by Michael Brooke and H. Lee Remmers. There he might have read about four types of multinational companies. Type A is the single-product company, usually small, reminiscent of the firm which Mr Kim joined. Here the links are said to be most straightforward, as contacts are maintained directly between chief executives at home and abroad. However, as it grows abroad, this type of company may change, with functional executives communicating with their counterparts overseas. Mr Kim soon became both chief executive and counterpart to the plant operator in Detroit, with the international division chief always in the picture, if ineffectually. Brooke and Remmers define type A as the least stable company, susceptible to mergers and broadening of product lines.

Type B is a company with a product group organization at headquarters and a geographical organization overseas. As the company facilities grow abroad, they become competitive with the export plans of the domestic product groups. They are represented in the home company's office by an international division which itself seems to compete with the product group exporters. There develops a '. . . prejudice against the foreign companies, a lack of interest, an unwillingness to help. So the block in communications arises: between the international division and the product management there is a clash of interest.'

Some companies have overcome the difficulties inherent in the type B organization by going to type C, wherein the international division is scrapped or held only as a liaison operation. Here, product groups operate with each other, from the home company's office directly to the field and back. This sidetracks communication from the head office to the field. It also exposes facilities abroad to control by product chiefs primarily interested in the prosperity of their home office units. (Perhaps Mr Kim's company was a type C?) Brooke and Remmers comment that: 'In these circumstances the foreign company may feel that it has all the disadvantages of an international company, such as slowness of decision, and no advantages. It has nowhere to turn.'

A final effort to solve the contradictions in types A, B and C is type D, which is the most complex scheme of organization and holds within it possibilities for more growth and for even more conflict. This combines product groups and geographical management. If the latter is stronger, under the shelter of an international division, product groups may be extended under the control of regional managers. If product groups are stronger, regional managers are reduced to an administrative role. In all probability most of the larger companies find, or seek, a compatible way of life in a shifting version of this plan for organization; the smaller companies settle for dominance in either the product group or control by an international division and its regional managers abroad.

One can sympathize with the manager abroad who does not know exactly what kind of company his employer is. The classifications of international organizations depend on the viewpoints of the classifiers. Howard Perlmutter, one of the best-known professors in the field of management education, has carved a career out of his classification of multinational companies; ethnocentric, where only executives from the nation of the parent company are considered competent to hold management positions anywhere; polycentric, where an almost over-enlightened attitude requires the company to put its management responsibilities abroad exclusively in the hands of local nationals (who themselves often become ethnocentric within the subsidiaries they manage); and geocentric, where 'the best man for the job' is selected at home or abroad regardless of his nationality. The exercise of classifying international organizations, which are usually in the process of change even while being classified, recalls the story of the elephant and the blind men, except that the elephant is bigger and the men occasionally blinder.

The effort must be made, however, and when the manager abroad has satisfied himself that he understands the organization employing him he is at the stage of continually guessing which of many possible shifts of direction the company is taking. Otherwise his part in long-range planning can become academic. Executives of the Interpublic Group of Companies discovered this one morning when they came to their offices to receive notice that the president of this group of fast-growing advertising agencies had been ousted in a carefully planned coup of the board, because the company plainly faced bankruptcy. The careers, investments in the company and jobs of some two thousand employees were immediately in danger and the five-year plans of the corporation and its subsidiaries were scrapped. The men abroad could be forgiven for being caught by surprise, although many were aware that all was not well at the centre of power. The fault was a simple one. The company was currently spending revenues that were projected as earnings ten years hence.

In a grinding, wrenching reorganization the new administration changed the company's course and saved the game, but not without inevitable damage at all levels. An organization which had apparently thrived on a policy of proliferation by acquisition and the splintering of divisions into companies, all serving each other until their deceptive sense of business growth was created, now had to eliminate its peripheral activities. It had to retract its more extended subsidiaries and reconstitute them into divisions serving the outside business community, and cancel long-range planning until the short-term operation could be made feasible in the view of clients and creditors.

As a survivor of that cataclysm I recalled how, years before as manager of the company's office in Buenos Aires, I had urged that we hedge against devaluation of the Argentine peso by investing blocked funds into the purchase of our office space. The answer from the home office pundits was swift: forget it, we were not in the real estate business. The Argentine branch has since lost a great deal through the effects of devaluation, the latest being in 1971, and has failed to profit from the soaring values of Buenos Aires' real estate. On the contrary, the company's entry in London followed local practice, perforce, by purchasing leases on office space, and the sale of these leases helped save the firm when the crash came.

The case is not exceptional. How many Rolls Royce men overseas were surprised in 1971? More unsettling to a man abroad and many at home is the question of what company he is working for. As mergers and acquisitions spread, he may be with Sheraton Hotels today, but the real policy-maker becomes I T&T tomorrow. Ciba may be battling Geigy for a share of the market one month and become Ciba-Geigy the next; and the long-range planners go back to the drawing-board along with those revising operations plans of the Dunlop–Pirelli combine, which is not exactly a combine. It is not surprising to find the following statement in an article by an executive of the American General Electric Company, describing that company's intricate responses to worldwide competition and its own growth:

'The departments or divisions are now responsible for a clear understanding of a global competitive arena in which their chief rivals assume the strangest identities: U.S. firms manufacturing abroad but competing in the home market; Japanese and European firms competing in the United States and in third countries; foreign firms joining forces with domestic companies to perform sales and services for foreign-made goods. Clearly no one can be on top of all these developments except those directly responsible for the business.

'. . . Certainly, management has not solved all the international organization problems. Perplexing questions, such as the co-ordination of the efforts of the foreign subsidiaries and U.S. departments in selling to third-country markets continue to rise.

'Yet there are many ways in which GE's international approach is more in tune with the times than it was ten years ago. At the same time it is still groping for today's right answers. It will undoubtedly be necessary to inject further changes so that the system better matches the capabilities of the company's managers as well as the economic realities of the world around them.'[1]

In the business environment as described, the manager abroad holds a position which is challenging in a two-dimensional sense. Other than

[1] *Columbia World Journal of Business*, November–December 1969.

the strangeness or unfamiliarity of his immediate environment, there are factors which importantly distinguish him from his domestic counterpart, and they strongly influence his performance as a strategist, as a planner.

The major inhibition on our man's accomplishments is the pattern of constraints imposed by his own company, which is why the question of its organization and its philosophy of operation is so important. If one is told, 'We will do the planning, you do the doing,' one's share of Napoleonic joys is ended. It is said and written that this will come about because of instant communications and almost instant travel. Decentralization will become a forgotten word when the men at headquarters can call an international conference on short-circuit television and end it with instructions to the troops on how to take the territory. This dismal fate is said to be partially imposed upon men abroad today by the telephone, Telex and the charms of first-class travel, tax-deductible, and enhanced by the companionship of the world's choicest and most charming stewardesses, with occasional delays at both ends of the trip for technical reasons. But the fact remains that the man in the bush knows more about it than someone shouting at him from a hovering helicopter. And even the most restrictive and carefully controlled companies must leave a wide range of options open to their men abroad if they mean to foster the quality of imagination as one of their attributes.

One such company, painstakingly organized but forcefully engrossed in its thrust toward growth, is Mead Johnson International. In its National Industrial Conference Board report on 'The Changing Role of the International Executive' the Mead Johnson country manager is reported to fulfil the following duties:

(a) Manages all Mead Johnson & Company operations in the country, bearing full responsibility for attainment of profit goals and all other approved objectives.

(b) Develops and recommends objectives, policies and plans for the country operation.

(c) Prepares and recommends consolidated annual budgets and proposed capital and extraordinary expenditure programmes.

(d) Develops and recommends major proposals affecting the subsidiary relating to legal, tax, financial and corporate matters.

(*e*) Establishes price structures and terms of sale for the country operation.

(*f*) Informs the vice-president and area director of all economic, political, legal and industry developments significantly affecting the subsidiary operation.

(*g*) Identifies, evaluates and recommends new products and product acquisitions for addition to the Mead Johnson line in (1) the country operations, (2) greater area operations or (3) elsewhere in the company's worldwide operations.

(*h*) Plans, approves, initiates and enforces improvements in the methods of organization and operation of the subsidiary and any of its components.

(*i*) Develops salary recommendations for his key executives; develops and approves other salary and wage structures.

The breadth of this charter opens wide areas for initiation in thought, analysis and recommendation. On nearly every point the manager is invited, in fact required, to be a human suggestion box for his parent company. But in point (*a*) there is a stern reminder of accountability, in a sweeping statement that in his function he is '. . . bearing full responsibility for attainment of profit goals and all other approved objectives.' Perhaps this is the rein held on all the remainder of his functions, for should his recommendations be accepted this is the reminder that he will be responsible for them. Otherwise – reread if you will – he is invited to propose budgets, administrative measures, new product development and nearly all adjustments affecting the operation of the business in his area, if he remembers point (*a*), which holds him responsible for the attainment of all profit goals and approved objectives. Passing ideas up the ladder is a stimulating exercise and perhaps one which should be encouraged, but being held responsible for their successful accomplishment if approved may inhibit the imaginative mind. Regardless, the adventurous executive abroad – and by definition the man abroad is adventurous – finds in such a directive room to flower.

Whether or not his parent company so explicitly outlines the responsibilities and opportunities assigned to its managers abroad, the fact of being in the field implies dimensions of challenge not intrinsic in domestic managership. Frederick Teague has listed four reasons why demands on the manager abroad are more severe, and they all bear strongly on his function as a strategist and planner.

1. A greater proportion of his energies are focussed on new ventures and new products.

2. There is a geographical and time distance between him and his home office.

3. He is operating outside the established organization, although within its directives.

4. Inevitably, because of a different environment, his management processes must be different, despite all efforts to make them cohere with the parent company philosophy.[2]

On the first point the fact that a company has extended its operations to another country constitutes a new venture. Unless it brings something new with it, there is little justification for having made the effort. It is taking a risk and usually it seeks compensation in a higher rate of return. When it stops being an innovator abroad, the international company loses its lead over the local national competitors. At that point its only advantage, now being equal as to product and operations, rests in its greater financial resources and cross-border flexibility, for which foreign critics attack it as parasitical rather than innovative since it presents unneeded and unwanted competition while contributing nothing new. Few multinational companies slip into such a position. Even the most cumbersome tend to hold the stimulus of a Research and Development department as a trump at the home base, a steady source of new product proposals. The manager abroad has the final responsibility of making the new products successful abroad.

This task is complicated because the products are so often not genuinely new, having been exploited in the home market and having, in many cases, reached maturity or the point of decline in the parent company territory. The parent company, having generated profits out of such products, usually assumes that it knows how to counsel their exploitation abroad. Too often, in the home view, 'abroad' is all one homogeneous territory. It is the task of the overseas manager to adapt the strategy of his parent company to the exigencies of his environment. He may have to recommend changes in production methods because

[2] *California Management Review*, Spring 1970.

of variations in supplies of raw materials and differences in the capabilities of his plant men. He may have to take issue on price structure because the local economy is at a less advanced stage or faces galloping inflation or operates under strict government planning. Local variables may require him to insist on changes in packaging and design. He may have to hold out for a different marketing and advertising approach and in doing so contend with the local branch of the advertising agency which serves the home office. He might find himself standing against the entire new product launch because he foresees failure in his market. At every step he encounters the choice of bending to the will of the parent company and returning final responsibility to the home office – ineffectually because parent company management will eventually say this is dodging his responsibility – or putting his job on the block by insisting on following his own counsel. These are extreme positions, often overcome by persuading the home office to accept the overseas point of view.

When major appliance manufacturers entered the post Second World War markets with washing-machines and dishwashers they encountered some astonishing reactions, and the sensitivity of managers abroad often prevented colossal marketing blunders. In Latin America and other male-dominated societies the expected appeal of these appliances as time-savers was negative. Women did not want to be caught escaping their duties, and in Argentina, for example, the manufacturers whose posters showed the liberated housewife letting her washing-machine do the work while she went to the cinema lost the market to the astute competitor who told her that the time saved could be applied to better care of her children and husband. As for automatic dishwashers, they have still to find a moral justification for purchase, even in Europe. The young housewife in France might accept one because it is modern, and her counterpart in Switzerland might be persuaded that it is more sanitary. But the market in both countries will be restricted as long as young couples are forced to move into housing with inadequate space for the machines.

One of the more catastrophic errors in international marketing stems from the parent company's belief that it can telescope the product life-cycle abroad. Its product, having survived the perils of the launching period at home, often with financial loss and considerable tinkering with both product and marketing strategy, is now at the profitable point of maturity and the belief holds that it can enter the foreign market at that stage. Years ago Campbell soups paid the price in discovering the fallacy in this line of reasoning in a U.K. sales campaign. The market was indifferent. The Americans sought to overcome its resistance with greater injections of advertising, but advertising of a type which assumed acceptance of the product concept. The acceptance was not there. It had to develop over a period of some years.

Later Polaroid made the same mistake, particularly in France. Polaroid had done brilliantly in America with a sparkling new product and advertising which explained it clearly while building public awareness and interest. The principal advertising medium used was television. When Polaroid had earned a sizeable share of the U.S. market, it compounded its success by introducing the Swinger, a lower-priced model for taking black-and-white pictures and developing them at a minimum speed of ten seconds. The parent company now saw the Swinger as the cure for its ills in France; Polaroid was still in a loss position there.

Heavy television advertising was impossible in France. With only two television chains and advertising time severely limited, no advertiser could mount a dominant television advertising campaign in France. The thinking at Polaroid seemed to reach the conclusion that price had been the obstacle to successful penetration of the French market, and that the Swinger would overcome that barrier. But the French were no more ready for the Swinger than they had been for the first Polaroid models because the educational groundwork had never been done, as it had in the United States. Further losses occurred despite mounting parent company pressure on its French manager. The battle continues, although the French public seems unaware of it.

Another type of new-product introduction allows the manager in the field a more exciting opportunity to demonstrate his strategic and tactical capacities. This occurs when a foreign country is selected as laboratory ground to test a product which later may become part of the company's international line. With no prior experience behind the product, and preconceptions at a minimum, the home office in this case is more willing to let its manager abroad carry out the necessary market research, base his recommendations on it and assume full responsibility for the tactical assault on the market. Even here, however, there are limitations. His strategy should not be so tightly tuned to local conditions as to make it impossible to evaluate the product's prospects in other markets. Coca-Cola's Fanta orange drink is a case in point. First introduced in Australia, it found a response which was later verified in Latin America and parts of Europe before it became part of the company's international arsenal. Now Brazil is the testing ground for a high-protein soft drink which may emerge as a boon to the heavily populated less-developed countries suffering from nutritionally unbalanced diets. The race for high-protein foods from new sources is on, with the petroleum companies testing their raw product for possibilities, and Nestlé and Esso combining forces on the venture. With 87 million children throughout the underprivileged world suffering from protein and calorie deficiencies the opportunity for a major contribution from technologically advanced international companies is great and growing. According to the World Health Organization, 'Malnutrition is not only a health problem. It is also a problem of human development, with all the consequences that this implies for social and economic progress in the world.' The overseas manager is on the front line of that battle, but strategy and logistics rest with parent companies and their R & D departments.

Futurologists discerning the advance of a computerized world, which will allow companies to locate plants wherever labour conditions are most favourable and to control them from their headquarters, seem to write off much of the responsibility now assigned to the outpost manager. This appears to lighten the load which geographical and time separation from the parent office now add to the field manager's role. Regardless, he will continue to be part of the planning process because his presence on the scene of production or marketing ensures that his feedback will become part of the input for computerized designs for operations.

Also, small companies may not become so thoroughly mechanized. More likely they will continue to establish branches abroad which are replicas, with local overtones, of the home company. And among them will be the proliferating service companies – in banking, insurance, advertising, management consultancy and so on – whose prime effort is to instill a person-to-person relationship with clients.

The time and distance separation further removes the field manager from the established pattern of organization at headquarters. It also thrusts him into environments which demand shifts in management style with a bearing on tactics and on planning. In the Eastern bloc economies, where Western firms may soon be allowed to establish facilities, state planning requires a different managerial attitude. Even France, in the West, is less of a free enterprise economy than the U.S., Britain or Holland. And in Japan, where business collaborates with a government which outlines and subtly guides a national economic trajectory, management must adapt not only to the national economic concept but to a different view of how companies should be administered. Home offices will continue to rely on men in the field who can make the necessary adjustments to these varying conditions while sending back the raw information for headquarters planning.

The planning process, like most managerial activities in the field, follows a company pattern which not unnaturally reflects the national traits of the headquarters company. Swiss and American companies tend toward a federalist view which the federal states of both might well have spawned. Not unlike the constitutions of their home countries, the charters of these companies arrogate certain rights to the parent offices and leave the rest to the discretion of their subsidiaries. The global plan, financial control and discretion over top personnel are headquarters decisions plus, lately, plans concerning the location and utilization of research and development. Very often central marketing concepts are also home office prerogatives. But day-to-day tactics, interpretation of headquarters concepts and application or adaptation of central directives are matters for the subsidiaries to decide. The federal idea prevails, with the home office playing the part of the central government and the subsidiaries acting the role of the cantons or states.

A British company too reflects in its way the ideas of government associated with the U.K. It may operate with an unwritten plan like Beecham's (Britain has no written constitution) and it seems to bumble its way through, as mystified observers have so often witnessed in the British method of confrontation with the most massive of problems. It usually is effective for the British company, as it has been for Britain, because the bumbling process usually turns out to be a way of concealing one's cards and is guided by ideas buried in history which the British understand well enough not to require repeated articulation.

An Italian company, like Italy itself, always carries the overtones of the Caesars. And the farther it moves away from the Caesars, like the

Italian government, the more it stumbles into a morass of indecisiveness. No great international Italian company can be entirely disassociated from its leading personality: Fiat and Agnelli, Olivetti and, Peccei Pirelli, for example. In their subsidiaries, Italian companies follow the pattern. They are usually led, or rather directed, by a brilliant, highly presentable personality, a dictator in his own business and a consummate diplomat in his dealings with key figures in his environment, including the officials of his host government. One strong but nearly invisible cord inhibits him: it is his response to the even stronger man in his parent company.

The Scandinavians, who tend toward management by committee, export their method to their field offices abroad. One may find a manager, but usually his decisions will be the result of discussions with his most trusted associates. Scandinavian Airlines is a classic example, its offices abroad usually including a Swede, a Norwegian and a Dane in the management circle and none is excluded from major decision-making meetings.

Allowing for different national management styles and for diverse national histories, the trend is towards central global planning based in varying proportions on proposals and information from the field. The aware manager abroad knows that he will be held responsible for carrying out the company programme. He will therefore want to have a vote in what that programme will be. In some firms this will be required of him, as in the American companies which swamp their men abroad with demands for periodic reports and commitments to medium-term plans. Rarely will an energetic field manager allow himself to be restricted to a reporting role; his chance to chart his future begins when the map is being drawn at the home company's office and if he withdraws at this point a subsequent success can be an annoyance to the chiefs who were not taken into his confidence, and a failure may be his alone. For his own good and that of his company he must be associated with his company's worldwide planning process.

Too many companies ignore the desirability of bringing their field managers into their total planning, looking on them as line tacticians assigned to carrying out but not developing strategies. Whether a company falls into this category often depends upon the degree of its centralization or decentralization, but certainly not upon a scarcity of considered advice on the matter from consultants specialized in international business. One such advisory service, Business International, in a volume entitled *Corporate Planning Today for Tomorrow's World Market*, has outlined suggestions that planning should not be too centralized. Its proposal for a 16-step procedure can be condensed as follows:

1. *Begin the planning process with a definition of what the company is.*

2. *Keep the plan flexible.* Furthermore, no plan should be so rigid that it puts line operators in a straitjacket. If a plan is so inflexible that it does not permit managers to seize on new ideas and explore new avenues of profit, it will be self-defeating. A plan which is not quickly adapted to changing conditions or which stifles managerial initiative can kill the spirit of a company's managers.

3. *Recognize that international planning is infinitely more complex than domestic planning.* International planning presents more alternatives and involves assessing a wider range of problems. Among other things, international planning puts added stress on political forecasting because of the enormous impact of politics – both national and international – upon world economics and business.

4. *Maintain a clear distinction between professional planners and line officers.* To the extent that the professional planning staff influences these basic goals and strategies it participates in high policy-making. But the tactical decisions of carrying out the plan must be left to the line officers.

5. *Keep plans in line with the people available to realize them.*

6. *Make manpower development the key item in the plan.* Importantly, management progression plans lose much of their effectiveness if, in their search for, and development of, leadership – including leadership of the parent company – they stop at the water's edge. For many companies the pool of lower-level managers from which future leadership can be drawn is larger outside the national borders of the parent company than it is within.

7. *Create a strategic long-range plan to supplement your medium-term plan.* Yet the principal aim and benefit of planning, in the view of many

51

companies, is to uncover problems before they occur and in time for action to be taken to avoid them. Obviously, medium-term plans of the type just described will not achieve that purpose. Hence the need for a strategic plan that looks ahead for problems (and opportunities) that demand action today but that would not be discerned in the absence of such a longer-range plan. Trends and events are now in motion which will dramatically change the business environment a decade and more away, and which require action today if the company is to survive and prosper in these later years.

8. *Combine 'top-down' and 'bottom-up' planning.* Division managers must know what the chief executive officer expects of them and the chief executive officer in turn must know what the divisions think they can accomplish. A key function of a planning department or planning manager is that of helping the division executives and the chief executive officer come to agreement on a plan based on a realistic appraisal of external conditions and corporate resources.

9. *Insure that the plan leads to immediate action.* To quote some experienced planners: 'The ball game in planning is programming.' A plan merely represents an expensive waste of time and money if it simply gathers dust in a file and is not put to work. A plan must rest solidly on the conviction that 'tomorrow is the cause, today is the result'. Or, in the vernacular, 'plan your work, then work your plan'.

10. *Create planning posts at various levels and work to fill them with competent people.* There is overwhelming agreement that professional planners do not in fact *create* the plan. In the final analysis, the only executives who can do this are the line operators responsible for the achievements of the plan's goals. But planning techniques are rapidly being developed into a science of themselves, especially with the introduction of computers.

Professional planners, by assisting line executives in the planning effort, can also keep those managers from devoting too much time and effort to planning. This is especially true at the subsidiary company level. Many subsidiaries of international corporations are, in reality, small businesses; their presidents or general managers must stay close to their customers.

11. *Improve planning inputs from the field.* Most companies find when they initiate medium-term planning that the projection and ideas received at headquarters are, at least initially, quite poor. But most companies would agree that the corporate headquarters should actively seek to orient divisions and subsidiaries to the value, purposes and techniques of planning and to educate line managers in how to carry it out. Furnishing this assistance in a formal way is essential.

12. *Integrate domestic and international financing.* Whether or not a company's international business is handled by an international division or conducted by product or geographic divisions, it cannot afford to plan for domestic operations in isolation from plans for other markets. The earth is simply shrinking too fast.

The most effective planning in these terms would consist of one global plan expressing a unified approach to corporate goals and objectives right from the start. But at the very least there must be complete integration of domestic and international plans at headquarters before either plan is finally adopted.

13. *Take steps to minimize the cost of planning.* Like everything else planning can get out of hand in terms of people, time and money unless it is carefully structured. The size of the planning department, the number of planners, the expenditure on information inputs, etc., must be carefully determined.

14. *Plan to improve the profitability of existing business.*

15. *Strengthen external environmental inputs in the plan.* In planning, most companies are quite strong in terms of the corporate information they programme into the plan – the quality and performance of existing products, cost of goods sold, etc. They are very much weaker in terms of weaving in external environmental information. Yet the pace of environmental change is blinding. The world is undergoing a metamorphosis.

16. *Concentrate on the chief executive officer as top planner.* The chief executive officer is the single most important element in planning. He can make or break the planning effort.

There is also the danger that he may apply 'domestic' criteria in his planning instructions as they apply to the international operations of his company. If he is not aware of the reality and significance of the world market, he may insist on the application of traditional, national standards of measurement, risk and profit that will stultify the planning effort.

Sensible suggestions, all sixteen of them. But if the manager abroad is to achieve the Aristotelian goal of happiness through the exercise of excellence, he may be forced to become an effective reminder to his company that the world is not only divided in space, but in time. The Ivory Coast may be sixty years behind headquarters; Sweden, forty years ahead. Or Sweden may be forty years ahead in some social concepts and twenty years behind in other technological areas. But the Ivory Coast may be hurtling forward at a breakneck speed – predictions are that GNP growth there will *slow* to a yearly rate of 10 per cent in 1972 – while Sweden may have reached a point of stagnation. Can a headquarters global plan overlook the different stages of growth of the diverse parts of the world and the different rates at which change is taking place? If it does, its five-year plan is a concoction of dreams and it has failed to use its managers abroad to the full extent of the awareness and sensitivity that should be bred into them.

Chapter 4

Administration –
Centralize or Decentralize?

Although an international company holds at headquarters the reins on central policy, finance, senior executives – and often R & D and product quality control – administration does not fall into a simple pattern either at headquarters or in the field. The central fact of multinational business is that it is multinational; therefore it operates in a multiplicity of environments and – in the varying stages of economic growth abroad – in a variety of changing points in time.

Students of international business, including the men who administer it, continue to seek the formula by which it should best operate; but environments refuse to stabilize and the rules cannot be frozen. General agreement is limited to recognition that the environment for international business is inconstant, and flexibility provides the most acceptable basis for confronting it.

An interesting attempt to develop this principle is made by Endel J. Kolde and Richard E. Hill, writing on 'The Conceptual and Normative Aspects of International Management'. They recognize at the start that

'... to be able to establish its goals and strategies rationally, a multinational firm must not only understand its environmental structure but also be sensitive to the sources and forces of change that constantly transform the patterns of incentives, impediments and rewards which define opportunities and provide the standards for managerial performance ... In sum, the cultural and institutional plurality of the international environment confronts management with a more diverse and complex reality which is the source and justification for international management as distinguished from management *per se*.

55

International or multinational management, therefore, may be defined as the direction of an enterprise in a plurality of national environments and institutional structures.'[1]

This effort to formalize such a general premise is followed by certain propositions which seek further to define an international management concept. The first proposition states that:

'The plurality and diversity of external factors make it necessary that any national or continental suborganizations of a multinational company possess the power to solve problems and issues which are peculiar to their domicile. Decentralization, therefore, is fundamental for international management.'

This precept is supported by four determinants:

1. 'Laws and public policies governing corporate behaviour and defining the limits of entrepreneurial freedom and action differ in countless respects. There are no two countries whose laws and policies are the same . . . Multinational decision-making, therefore, lacks the common system of laws and principles which in the national realm serve as basic ground rules for behaviour.

2. 'Industrial relations also require national treatment. Few unions cross international boundaries. Each country has its own labour organizations and policies regarding wages, working conditions and the settlement of disputes.

3. 'Public relations are another function which often require local decisions. The behaviour of the executive within the country is an important determinant of public opinion.

4. 'Economic and market conditions, too, require diverse approaches of management. That people in different countries have different tastes, different levels and patterns of income, and different consumption habits are facts too obvious to dwell on. From these derive the different criteria for product characteristics, for advertising appeals, distribution channels and marketing policies.'

Support for the second proposition – 'The environmental plurality of a multinational firm tends to induce an analogous plurality in its

[1] *Academy of Management Journal*, June 1967.

internal structure' – brings in full recognition of the indigenous manager whose numbers are increasing:

'In the new ex-colonial countries, executive expectations and decision-making behaviours represent a bewildering maze of different patterns, most too little studied to permit any substantive generalizations. To a certain degree the managerial patterns of the previous colonizing power are usually evident; in Burma things are done as in Britain, rather than as in France or the U.S.; in Indonesia the model is Dutch and in Algeria it is French. But this is not saying much. In all these countries the colonial heritage is submerged under indigenous forces which engender new and distinct administrative systems, most of them highly autocratic, often even militaristic in character . . .

'It would seem doctinaire folly for a multinational corporation (American) to attempt to impose upon its foreign-based entities any Americanized organization structure or leadership system. At best such an attempt would alienate the indigenous managers from corporate goals and stifle their effectiveness; at worst it could give the company a neocolonialist image and incite the negative political reactions which can thwart its markets and encumber its growth . . . Decentralization can be a powerful motivator for indigenous managers.'

The next proposition reverts to the powers of the parent company and seeks to formalize them by stating:

'To function effectively as an organic whole in its pluralistic international environment, the multinational corporation must co-ordinate all decisions which transcend in application or consequence any national sub-entity of the company.'

Taking for granted the usually centralized areas of finance, basic policy and top management control, Kolde and Hill reach into some functional areas to support this proposition. Their argument is that:

'Co-ordination presumes that there is a central purpose and a power to pursue – centralization. That the overall objectives and strategy must be decided on the multinational level needs hardly to be emphasized. But equally important, and usually much more difficult, is the co-ordination of specific functional aspects of the multinational structure. Here the arguments for decentralization and centralization are on a collision course.'

Functional areas referred to include marketing, when different subsidiaries serve the same client; finance, in intercompany dealing; and personnel training guidance.

Finally the discussion is summarized with an umbrella proposition stating that:

'Multinational management should be conceived as consisting of two vertical spheres; (1) a nationally and culturally decentralized base-structure designed to deal with pluralistic conditions through strong autonomous sub-entities on the national and local levels, and (2) a centralized superstructure to guide and co-ordinate the organization as a whole on the international and multinational levels.'

Such discussions provide a useful framework for the multinational companies and their managers abroad in designing their organizations and administrative formulae. Certain principles survive, despite the variable environments surrounding international business, but they are not rigid. Concepts of centralization and decentralization vary from company to company and within the same company, from time to time.

I clearly recall a meeting with an overseas manager of an international petroleum company in one of the Latin American countries. This was a company whose ideas on centralization and decentralization changed with each switch in the parent company's top management. It was now following a proclaimed move toward greater decentralization, even to the territorial divisions within each country in which it operated.

We had, as managers of our companies, come to an agreement on a plan involving both companies.

'I hope your division managers from the provinces will go along with this programme, I said as I prepared to leave the manager's office.

'There won't be any trouble about that,' he replied. 'We have a meeting scheduled for this afternoon.'

'Good luck, then. Some of those fellows are a bit stubborn, especially under your decentralization programme.'

'Don't worry about that,' he said. 'We'll just have to centralize for about half an hour.'

This was done and there was agreement on the plan. Of course my friend had acted counter to headquarters directions but one could be certain that if the incident had been reported at a board of directors' meeting there would have been a few grunts and smiles and no further notice taken. With so much leeway and change in the parent company's approaches to the administration of their international affairs, they are rarely severe about how their managers abroad interpret the rules. It is probably in this area of administration that the home office tries hardest to formalize its business, and fails most often; but the failure is in itself a success because it reflects flexibility. And it is probably in the same area that the manager in the field has most room for creative implementation of his company's policies. An overview of how some companies pattern their international organization stresses this point.

One of the most successful and experienced of these firms is Philips of Eindhoven, a multiproduct, multiservice worldwide sprawl with subsidiaries ranging from its powerful, nearly autonomous, entity in the U.S. to minor sales agents in the provinces of some of the poorer countries. Its basic organization borrows from the business philosophies of various cultures. On the executive level there is clearly a participative tone to Philips operations, encouraging face-to-face discussions and maintaining a company fleet of airplanes to facilitate them. Yet there is a strong element of centralization in the Philips organization.

It is headed by a board of management in Eindhoven, with a president who is assisted by three vice-presidents. This group meets frequently, as does a supervisory board of directors. There are twelve product divisions in charge of overall policy, each responsible for the manufacture, development and marketing of its group of product lines. Responsible to the board of management and available to the product divisions and foreign subsidiaries is an operating service-group concerned with finance, legal affairs, personnel, marketing and sales planning, industrial and technical information, general manufacturing and efficiency studies, and purchasing and manufacturing of production machinery.

Abroad there are twelve to fifteen regional bureaux, each of which represents the subsidiaries within its region and is the channel of communication between them and Eindhoven. Budgets, accounts, new products and pricing are matters requiring home office approval, although the details in each area (except accounting systems) are left largely to the subsidiary; in matters of advertising and labour relations the degree of autonomy is much greater.

An alternative is the 'shared responsibility' concept of Miles Laboratories. This is an effort to define profit responsibilities both in the home office and in the field. A written policy statement on 'International Operations Organization' outlines the idea. The parent company's product divisions are '. . . responsible on a global basis for profit down to the level of divisional contribution, i.e. after charging all expenses directly identified with divisional activity' whereas the subsidiaries are '. . . responsible for profit at the level of net income, i.e. after charging all local divisional expenses plus general administration, interest, taxes and other expenses incurred in running the entity.'

Miles maintains two channels of communication between the home office and the subsidiary, with one flowing between the home product division and the appropriate department heads in the field on technical matters. Also by this channel, communication moves between the home office corporate services (legal, personnel, etc.) and the assigned officers abroad. By the other channel the home office communicates directly with the manager abroad on matters concerning the profit plan.

There are so many diverse concepts of administration of international companies that the classic organization charts are classic no longer, and degrees of centralization and decentralization are infinite.

Pirelli of Italy has been particularly creative in patterning its international operations. The starting point for its high degree of decentralization is its international corporation which is located in Basle, Switzerland, where it achieves a high financial potential and where its site in a neutral country avoids many political complications. Pirelli International is the largest stockholder in its Italian parent company. The parent company maintains control over technical and managerial matters and the international office in Basle supervises financial operations abroad. However, the management plan at Pirelli leaves all possible operations to the managements of its subsidiaries; for example, by requiring profit and loss reports from them only every three months.

Subsidiaries are requested to structure themselves according to the parent company organization, which includes three managing directors who report to a chairman. One handles staff functions, the other two are in charge of product lines. But fundamentally the company limits

its control over the international division to the technical and financial levels and the international office in Basle encourages local decision making on the part of its subsidiaries. Notably it leaves them free to adapt to local environmental constraints or opportunities.

Another multinational company which manages its cross-border operations through a separate international firm is IBM. Its international control is vested in the IBM World Trade Corporation in New York. The proliferation of manufacturing facilities and development laboratories overseas has created special organizational problems for IBM and its World Trade Corporation is the answer to most of them.

Since the overseas country companies are so strongly involved in the firm's worldwide manufacturing plan, World Trade has extended its control through strong regional or area offices. Decision making is delegated to the extent possible, but within a system of checks and balances. Customer relations are largely handled by the country subsidiaries. Essentially, basic research and product development are integrated worldwide functions combining the company's domestic divisions and World Trade.

World Trade manages its business in 106 countries through four area offices and two regional branches which subdivide the Far East area. The area offices are considered as extensions of the World Trade headquarters. Its country managers have major management responsibility except for finance, product development, external government contracts, and cross-border engineering co-ordination; however, even in the proscribed functions their counsel is sought by headquarters.

The requirements of a diversified company call more emphatically for new approaches to worldwide organization and administration. Sperry Rand is a case in point. The company has product lines in business machines, instrumentation, control systems, farm machinery, hydraulics and consumer goods, some of them having been independent businesses before being acquired by Sperry Rand. Some formerly had international divisions, others were totally global companies. Accordingly, each of Sperry's nine product divisions handles its own international operations, some with international departments, some without.

What might have become an unmanageable degree of decentralization has been overcome at Sperry by establishing umbrella companies

61

which join the subsidiaries within countries abroad. The umbrella company opens communications between the otherwise independent divisions and in each country presents a unified Sperry Rand image to the public. The managing directors of the subsidiary companies constitute the board of directors of the umbrella company, which has a separate chairman whose entire staff consists of a secretary-treasurer.

The long arm of finance reaches through to the subsidiaries since they join in making a budget for the umbrella company which must be approved by U.S. corporate headquarters.

Sperry Rand also uses the classic instrument of regional offices, each of which supervises the product divisions in its area. For example, the Vickers or Remington Rand subsidiaries in a region are brought under the Vickers or Remington Rand regional office which has profit responsibility as well as administrative responsibility for co-ordination. The regional office, however, does not cut off direct communication between subsidiaries and product division headquarters.

Increasingly one comes upon examples that support the idea that each company develops its own structure to suit its own situation, rather than following a single theory of international corporate organization. American Standard is a multiproduct company with one product division which heavily outweighs the others. To give the three other product lines more freedom for growth, it put the international vice-president in charge of the major division, plumbing and heating, and cut the others loose with their chiefs. This also leaves room for major acquisitions, either to be absorbed into the existing four divisions or to constitute new divisions. In contrast, American Cyanamid, which also contains diverse product lines retains international control through an international centre and geographical area subdivisions. However, within this structure the product lines are separated and report to product division managements.

Charles Pfizer & Company, in a similar business, follows different procedures tending toward greater decentralization. Its export department has evolved into Pfizer International, a wholly-owned subsidiary, which conducts its business through independent management centres and an international staff. Like the parent company, Pfizer International has four product businesses: pharmaceuticals, agricultural products, chemicals and consumer products. It also has four management centres, in Brussels, Nairobi, Coral Gables and Hong

Kong. They are highly independent and handle all decisions except those concerning overall company policy.

To this somewhat classic structure is added a feature that particularly meets Pfizer objectives: four product directors, one for each product line, who report to the president of Pfizer International. They are functionally responsible for all international sales and sales-related operations and they assume co-ordination with the domestic parent through regular meetings with its product managers.

Even more strongly inclined toward the product group structure is KZO (Netherlands) which operates through six product divisions. This meets the needs of the two companies which merged to form KZO and it leaves the company free for further growth through acquisition. The company units meet at the top in a supervisory board which includes heads of the six divisions, the company president, the chief of staff, a vice-chief of staff, and the research co-ordinator. However, all day-to-day decisions, again with the exception of finance, are left with the six product division managers.

There is recognition at KZO that a degree of co-ordination can strengthen each of the separate divisions and the company has established regional staff committees to recommend sales and investment opportunities for the product divisions in different areas. Each committee can also suggest that certain product groups move toward apparent opportunities in various regions.

Other multinational companies prefer to establish their management communications along functional rather than product group or regional lines. Often these are smaller companies or they sell fewer products or they may have a number of licensees and joint venture partners. The functional structure allows a relatively small management group to control specific functions such as finance, manufacturing, sales and development. Often a company whose management group has worked together for many years will tend toward the system of controlling the field functionally, lawyer to lawyer, controller to controller, etc., despite the danger of fouling lines of reporting. More often this type of company will be European rather than American.

One such firm is SKF (Sweden), maker of ball bearings, whose business has soared since 1957. It has had to change its organization from the time when its major factory and corporate management were in the same headquarters, and it has chosen a functional design whereby marketing, planning, finance, personnel, legal, sales, public relations, engineering and research, and manufacturing services report to its top-management group. All production centres everywhere also report directly to top management. Only in sales is there a regional line of reporting with four regional managers, for Eastern Europe, the Andean countries, Central America, and the Far East, controlling sales development in those areas. The secret to co-ordination is in the top-management group of veterans of the company whose informal relationship with each other and knowledge of the company makes the system work.

Such variations on three themes of international company organization – geographic, functional, and based on product group – are endless, as each company seeks to gear its operations for the best use of its resources, the most skilful exploitation of its opportunities, and the best stance from which to expand profit and promote growth. It would be difficult to find two companies with exactly parallel organization charts and if one made such a discovery, investigation would show that they were interpreted differently. For example, the distinction between line and staff responsibilities is often blurred and consciously so.

Atlas Copco (Sweden) exemplifies originality in its assignment of line and staff work. It has three worldwide product divisions and an international sales company. But because 90 per cent of sales are generated outside of Sweden, the international sales company picks up responsibility for the other 10 per cent in the domestic market.

To balance tension between the international sales company and the product divisions, both profit-responsible, the company has established a third group, a functional marketing staff which develops policies, long and short-term goals, marketing methods, and environmental intelligence, and arbitrates these matters between the product divisions and the sales company. While providing a staff service to the product divisions it takes a line position in reviewing performance of the sales company and its branches.

Monsanto puts staff men in positions that cross other line responsibilities. There is a unified corporate staff which includes major functions, with administration as the key. Heads of corporate staff service report to administration, which includes international staff executives. In the regions, staff executives report directly to their corporate counterparts. This may place some pressures on field managers whose staff men are reporting past them to headquarters.

Abex (U.S.) assigns a different role to its international department, giving it line responsibility for exports while it acts as staff service on foreign licensing and new business for product divisions. It also investigates possible new ventures abroad, as a service; but it has no administrative co-ordination role in connection with the subsidiaries.

Within such a complex of organizational possibilities, the manager in the field usually has all the freedom he can handle. His company has a chart and he must respect it; but the chart was probably different a few years ago and will change, and is changing, as the company acquires new resources and adapts to a changing scene.

It is the living scene abroad that the manager in the field must evaluate from day to day; no organization can do that. It is the manager abroad who must determine how to adapt the corporate practices of his company to the local scene; no set of regulations can tell him how to accomplish this. This does not mean that he is free to limit his viewpoint to his immediate surroundings or those of the country or area to which he has been assigned. How he operates can affect his company globally as well as locally; a creative triumph or a miserable blunder will have repercussions on his company managers' future activities abroad. Janus-like, he must look closely about him and into the distance simultaneously.

It is not expected of a manager abroad that he religiously apply the company's organization chart to the office over which he presides. In most cases this would be a ridiculous effort for three reasons: the peculiarities of his immediate environment, the resources of his office, and the sections of the global company plan which are assigned to his office.

In assessing his environment, he would first do best to attempt an understanding of its social structure, for this is the determinant of how a society will react to change, challenge or stimulus. Is the basis of security the organization? And does 'the organization' mean, as in Japan, the family and the company; or as in other countries, the state; or as in some societies, a professional or technical grouping of lawyers, engineers, accountants; or as elsewhere, the university, the club, the social class?

Having gained a proper insight into the social infrastructure, the manager can better assess how he will translate the company's administrative policies in his own plant or office and better predict its reactions to his initiatives. He edges his way toward the role that will make him most effective. He can be detached and Olympian. He can be parental, the father figure. He can surround himself with a management committee to reflect a participative feeling. He can be a shirt-sleeve manager who strolls about the plant and learns the first names of most of his men. Each role may have its place in the appropriate setting. But if the role assumed is patently a contradiction of the manager's inner self, its falseness will become evident and nullify the effort.

Japanese companies moving overseas have quickly realized that headquarters principles are not exportable. They are aware of the language barrier, one that exists for most cross-border companies; however, many deny its importance as managers come increasingly to rely on bilingual secretaries. They are concerned about distributor relationships because their companies are giants at home, with no distribution problems, but are small overseas where distribution patterns are different. Most shocking are the differences in employee attitudes. 'In Japan', as one such manager has said, 'every employee thinks he is a potential manager. So he behaves like one early in his career. A Japanese worker will postpone his vacation or split it up into small periods, when there is work to be done. In France such things are unthinkable.' And elsewhere.

Another Japanese manager abroad says: 'In France the employee population is far more independent and mobile. A worker will not do much more than the limited task he is given. Even then you must supervise him to make sure it is done at all.' And elsewhere.

Therefore the Japanese home office must allow its managers abroad to make, to the extent possible, the adjustments necessary in keeping with the home office precepts. It realizes, however, that afield matters will not be arranged as they are at home.

How can they be? The administrative officer of an American branch in Hamburg – a German – once told me,

'We are confused when we receive communications from New York that say, "We suggest that you do this," or "We recommend that you do that," or "We would advise that you do the other thing." To that our reaction is "Thank you for your suggestion, recommendation and advice – we will go ahead as we have planned." Then a storm blows up. Why don't Americans say what they want? We would understand perfectly if we received messages saying, "We demand that you do this, that or the other." "We require that this be done." '

Recognizing the distance in human equations from the home office to the field, most multinational companies are quite ready to accede to the devices of their field managers in administrative matters as long as they are successful in fulfilling requirements of major policy and the budget. In fact, without saying so the home office would usually rather not be asked for decisions on administrative matters. The request always calls for a place on the agenda of a home office management meeting, usually an embarrassment because no one present knows much about the subject and all have to appear knowledgeable. The best way to appear in the know is to veto the motion, realizing that the others present cannot defend it; so a perfectly good idea from the field is rejected. It is best for the manager abroad not to plague the home office for confirmation of his initiatives! They will be accepted if he is doing well, on balance. If he does badly, all his decisions will be held against him.

This chapter concerns administration and that is a grey area in itself. Administration is one of the business words that can embrace too much and should include only the structuring of the company and how a manager makes it work within that structure. But consider these examples. Are they administrative? If not, what are they?

In Argentina expatriate managers of foreign offices, especially those from the United States, were usually annoyed by the local custom of taking two and a quarter hours for lunch. The Argentines contended that they needed this interval to go home, have the big meal of the day, generously washed down with wine, and get back to the office – usually after a fifteen-minute nap. The American managers filled in the time at their club, often spending too much of it at the bar. The resultant overeating and overdrinking meant a pretty dull performance back at work at least until three-thirty in the afternoon.

Different administrative attempts to solve the problem failed to break the system. An outright order to cut the luncheon interval to one hour met protests that personnel could not afford downtown restaurant prices and would have to be granted generous wage increases or they would leave – en masse.

One manager sought a solution within the system. As the warm summer weather came on he spread the idea that the staff might like an earlier afternoon closing hour during the two hottest summer months. There was immediate interest and when the thought had taken hold, he further suggested this might be arranged by changing to one hour for lunch during that period. He then suggested an office vote on the subject and a majority accepted the new summer hours.

The experiment having turned out to be a pleasant experience for most, the next year the manager offered to extend the summer hours to a four-month period and this, too, was accepted. By the fourth month the staff had learned to take light snacks for the noontime meal downtown, costing little more than the transportation home and back to the office. Even more to their liking, they enjoyed sports, movies, and amorous excursions in the late afternoon before going home. In the fourth month the manager proposed that the new hours be retained all the year around and this, too, found acceptance.

The measure had taken two years to bring about but dissidence and the loss of good employees had been avoided. True, office hours were a bit shorter but the performance of the staff in the afternoon was immensely improved over the former days when they had become tired in the city traffic and had returned swollen and fuzzy-headed to the office. The administration had worked within the culture and brought about a beneficial change. The home office was unaware that there had been a problem or that it had been solved.

That office continued to have another problem, however. The young man who had been put in charge of the traffic department responded to his promotion by consistently coming in each morning a half hour after the office opened. Finally the manager decided to confront the young man with the defect.

'You used to come in on time. Why not now – especially with a department under your responsibility?'

'That's just it,' replied the youth, 'I have to show my prestige to the others in the department.'

The experiences of three different branches of an international advertising agency well illustrate how the application of local administrative creativity can solve problems in the field by taking measures not included in home office policy, but which avoided worry at headquarters. The field offices are in London, Geneva, and Lima, Peru.

The London office is sizeable, with over three hundred employees. Some years ago it was feeling competitive pressure from the small creative shops springing up in London which claimed to offer advertisers more exciting work and direct contact with the people doing the job. This had been going on in the United States for some time, causing problems for the large advertising agencies there also. The home office of this particular agency was toying with the idea of decentralizing, setting up full service sections, each like a small advertising agency, each to compete in this way with the small 'hot shops'. But the process of making this change was cumbersome in such a large company, which had some 1,200 employees in New York. There was much writing of memoranda on the subject, but no action.

The London office decided to move ahead on the idea. It tore out the partitions in the office space it was occupying and restructured a group of offices into a series of 'living rooms', each containing an art director, a copywriter, and an account executive. In some cases there would be a television executive also. Each cell decorated its office space as it wished. Each one also had a small separate space into which a worker could hide away for isolated concentration. Each separate group handled its own accounts. The central services of the agency remained apart but available: research, media purchasing, accounting, production, the library and – the management. The organization chart was redrawn with a series of circles surrounding a central circle, as replacement for the former pyramid. Clients received the change with enthusiasm, particularly when they saw the calibre of creativity within the agency improving and when they were able to deal directly with the people constructing their campaigns. The home office, for its part, was stimulated to move ahead with a similar plan, following the initiative in the field.

In Geneva, this company's branch embarked on a business principle quite contrary to home office precepts. It decided to specialize on sales promotion rather than concentrate on the use of the traditional advertising media, press, radio, and television.

In this case the parent company protested, pointing out that sales promotion was usually a losing activity for advertising agencies. In most cases advertisers preferred to keep this type of work in the house, and in others clients might want the service but were not prepared to pay adequately for it, often believing that the usual commissions from the traditional media should cover the agency's costs for this type of work.

The Geneva management pointed out that in Switzerland there are very few advertising accounts large enough to support an agency business dealing only with the mass media and that in the psychological atmosphere of business as practised in Switzerland nobody expected to receive either a product or service without making full payment.

Although headquarters disagreed, the Geneva management was able to draw out the controversy while it proceeded with its plan. The results were startling. The agency pre-empted a service area for itself which its competitors had overlooked. It was able to accept smaller accounts, with most funds put into sales promotion work, and it found little or no resistance to charges for such work although these charges often exceeded the income which use of the classic media might have yielded, while still adhering to the Swiss scale of charges. Finally, because it had decided to make sales promotion its speciality, it did the job well and clients received full value. Profits in the small Swiss office far exceeded those in many of the company's other branches.

The third administrative deviation occurred in Lima, Peru, not a rich market for advertising service nor a sophisticated one in the practice of advertising. The international advertising agency had an office there because a strong international client demanded its presence to serve its own affiliate. Under such circumstances an international service company grudgingly accepts a loss on its field operation to keep the client elsewhere. But it does not forego the usual home office pressure on the field manager for best possible financial performance. Often this executive finds himself in an ulcerous position, not only because the market is poor while the clients remain exigent, but because he is tied to certain parent company practices while his local competitors are free to improvise. This is particularly true where charges, commissions, and deals are involved. The international company with international clients or customers must meet certain financial standards even in its backwater branches. But the local competitors suffer no such restrictions.

This was true in Lima. Aggravating the problem was the requirement that the branch there be staffed as well as possible to serve the international clients, even though there might not be enough work to keep its creative personnel busy. After worrying over this problem, and repeatedly explaining it to the home office when it glowered at his profit and loss statements, the manager decided to make his own move.

He fired the art studio staff. He then offered the group its former office space and the general office services plus a guarantee of a certain amount of work if they wished to return on a free-lance basis. In their free time the artists could handle work for companies which were not clients of the agency, providing they were not competitive with the agency's clients and on condition that a percentage of the fees earned should revert to the agency. Not having heard of such a plan before, the home office felt constrained to silence. But when the Lima studio underwent a metamorphosis from a loss department to a profit centre, the parent company not only applauded the Lima initiative but advised other small branches to follow its example.

There are occasions, of course, when a bright-eyed manager in the field might become over enthusiastic in his creative approaches to administration. Personally, I encountered one such case on a supervisory trip to my company's office in Santiago, Chile. Having gone through the usual motions of take the office's pulse and blood pressure, I was preparing to return to Buenos Aires when the manager asked if I would join him on a short trip to the nearby port of Valparaiso. Chile is, or was, a charming country and a trip anywhere in it had its appeal. So I consented.

Once established in our hotel, the manager asked me to join him on a visit to a nearby office. It was then about six o'clock in the evening. A sense of misgiving began to gnaw at my mood of content. It increased as the elevator reached the seventh floor and it burgeoned into full bloom as we walked into an office half filled with joyous young men and women who seemed to be preparing a celebration.

'What's this?' I asked warily.

He offered me a cigarette, lit it deferentially, and answered, 'It's our new office in Valparaiso.'

'What the hell?' I exploded. 'Who authorized you to open an office in Valparaiso?'

'We have clients who want it. I've told you that.' He had, but I had asked him not to make the move. 'Didn't you receive my memo?' he asked. There was no memo but the query provided a face-saving escape for both of us – or alternatively I could fire him. But José was a good manager with a remarkably good record for building a profitable office.

'The memo must have been delayed in the mail,' I said. 'When are you planning to open the office? Maybe there's time to get New York authorization.'

José looked at his watch. 'In about forty minutes,' he replied. 'The Mayor of Valparaiso is coming for the ceremony. Then you make a speech.'

'I make a speech?'

He nodded. 'In Spanish,' he affirmed. 'They don't speak much English here.'

I saw a small bar being arranged. 'José,' I said, 'Give me a drink. And after that one, give me another.' As he started toward the bar, I shouted desperately to him, 'You know we could both be fired for this!'

José returned smiling and handed me a scotch and soda. We were not fired. José had a good record and I did also. A few years later the Valparaiso office closed down. But fortunately Santiago and José were still going strong – and as decentralized as ever.

Chapter 5

The Manager and the Money

The world of international finance is one of the most complex of contemporary business cultures. Governments become engulfed in its morass. Companies stumble into its traps. Speculators seek, and sometimes find, brilliant opportunities glinting among the threads of its web.

The world of cross-border finance breeds in profusion experts to explain and solve its problems. There are specialists in exchange, others on taxes, others on hedging, barter, and swaps, more on government and corporate securities, yet more on the location and use of sources of funds, and more still in the crucial sector of the expeditious management of cash resources. All share the condition that the situations which they analyse are constantly in flux, and they must continually attempt to predict the patterns which they will shape in the future.

Treasurers of international companies must thread their way through all these areas of expertise and spend all their time, and that of their advisors, at the task. Company managers abroad can hardly be expected to do likewise and still attend to their other responsibilities.

As we continue to discuss the relationships with his home office of the multinational man abroad we are required to look at, but not enter, the labyrinthine world of finance so important to both. We propose, then, to confine ourselves to sketching four broad subdivisions of this immensely intricate subject:

1. *The reporting functions of the manager.* In no area are the reporting duties of the manager abroad more precisely established. It is worth asking, however, whether this very precision, while aiding the home office treasurer, does not frequently cut off a potential source of productive information.

2. *The home office treasurer's panoramic view.* Unless the manager abroad understands that in the field of finance the home office has, or should have, a worldwide view, then his work in a particular locality will not make a maximum contribution.

3. *The special financial functions and opportunities of multinational companies.* Of all the types of expertise, with which multinational companies are credited or blamed, finance stands on a rung no lower than R & D, technology or management. The resources on which such companies may draw are often their point of competitive advantage over local firms, and their ability to move funds around the world can shore up tottering economies, although they can just as easily pull the plug on shaky currencies. Most nations seek the multinational company's financial contributions, while secretly wondering whether they are opening their doors to the Devil when they admit it.

4. *How the manager abroad can increase the value of his financial reporting.* If he is to be a robot responding only to instructions from the home office treasurer, the field of finance offers no opportunity for imaginative participation in the multinational workings of his company. Not many companies have devised techniques for making the reporting of their managers abroad stretch beyond the formalities; but a few managers have, and others can. They do this with a deep awareness of the difference between their status and that of the manager of a domestic branch.

The manager of a domestic division of a firm operates under a relatively stable set of financial constraints and opportunities. Except for local county, state, province and municipal taxes, well known to headquarters, his tax structure is predetermined, and the wrangle about it goes on at headquarters. He deals in the same currency as the rest of his firm and has no options concerning it. Interest rates and sources of funds are in the realm of the central treasurer's office. This manager, within the borders of his homeland, is often authorized to act as a controller over the division assigned to him. He has no treasury function. He is truly a reporter, and the manner of his reporting is established at the home office. Whether he reports daily, weekly, monthly or quarterly, or at all these periods, is decided at headquarters. The home office also decides what he reports and the forms on which his reports are to be received.

The manager abroad lives in a far more complex world. To be sure, his company usually tries to overcome the variables surrounding him by prescribing clear limits over his financial prerogatives and by defining the content of what it wants to hear from him regarding finance, as well as the form his reports should take. In doing so, headquarters attempts to relegate its manager abroad to the role of reporter, telling him (to the extent possible) how to control his business and how to return information about the results obtained. This is natural enough. The home office treasurer responsible for six to sixty balance sheets and profit and loss statements abroad, and called upon for periodic succinct reports to a steely-eyed board, is forced to simplify his relationship and communications with the overseas offices. He must seek a common financial language for all the offices to use. He must schedule the flow of information and he must have the security of knowing that none of the offices abroad can go beyond certain limits in managing their money. In fact, it is not their money; the funds belong to the corporate office and its stockholders. Occasionally, he finds it necessary to remind the field of this. This brings about an attitude which can be stultifying to the manager abroad, while curbing his usefulness to the company in an area vital to its survival. That this absurdity persists is reflected in a recent survey[1] of multinational companies concerning their delegation of financial responsibilities to managers abroad. The companies are not named.

Company A states: 'Local management operates under instructions from headquarters and has little authority for financial decisions.' However, 'Local managers make suggestions and recommendations.' Also, 'All borrowing by subsidiaries is subject to approval.'

Company B: 'International money management is rigidly controlled by headquarters; collections are made by the subsidiary and reported to headquarters . . . If a subsidiary needs new capital, headquarters makes the decision.'

Company C: 'Management of funds is generally centralized at corporate headquarters . . . The corporate treasurer invests at best yields obtainable internationally.'

[1] Herbert C. Knortz, 'The Job of the International Financial Manager', *Management Review*, September 1969.

Company D '... has centralized cash management and controls on a worldwide basis, covering both its U.S. and foreign operations ... Overall responsibility and decision-making rests with the general manager of international affairs, who is also the corporate treasurer.'

Company E introduces a new dimension. Because of its success abroad '... the sheer size of its worldwide operations and the magnitude of the individual foreign subsidiaries have forced wide decentralization and delegation of authority and responsibility to local management ... All operating subsidiaries are considered entities in themselves and in full control of their financial management ... Each subsidiary has its own financial programme and prepares an annual forecast. The report is submitted to headquarters but does not need its approval, although headquarters can raise questions and suggest changes ... Corporate management emphasizes the development of good local managers as the best way to achieve good results.' Whether company E's success is a result of such policies or a producer of them is not reported.

Company F: 'Local management has standing instructions to remit directly to headquarters all accumulated funds not needed for immediate use ... Headquarters closely reviews all reports, but delegates to local management relatively wide powers, particularly over bank accounts and local borrowing.'

Company G has moved much of its financial management function abroad, centralizing it in its London office. 'Local management submits monthly cash forecasts to the London central treasury office and to U.S. headquarters.'

Company H does likewise, with Brussels acting as the control point.

It is apparent that the survey concentrated on the question of cash management, but the responses indicate corporate policies as they affect all facets of financial management. In general, there would seem to be small basis for opposing the principle of centralized financial control; however, one reserves approval of application of this principle if it operates in such a way as to convert the manager abroad into a reporting machine. In this case both the company and the man lose effectiveness. Although the company should seek to avoid such a situation, it will often fall to the manager's personal ingenuity to find the remedy.

Except in the toughest of companies, remedies can be found, but before seeking them the manager abroad should understand the weight of his corporate treasurer's responsibility. For a growing business, not all the advantages and disadvantages of international life stem from its financial dealings; but many do. And their manipulation is the corporate treasurer's job. Other books deal with the benefits multi-national companies bring to nations seeking infusions of capital, technology, stimulus for their own industries, and increasing exports. Equally, they describe the irritation of countries which feel that multi-national companies, having made their initial investment – often on the favourable incentive terms offered to entice them – use the flexibility of their international status to overcome local competition with their greater access to funds and research, and to evade taxes with inter-company transfer pricing that holds profits down in high-tax countries while shifting them to low-tax nations. The multinational companies are also criticized for balancing their exports to suit their own global profit-goals rather than those of the host country in which they operate. Other factors press on the multinational firm, as we know. The rate of interest on capital, for instance, and the prospect of devaluation or re-valuation of the host country's money, the oncoming of inflation in the host country, or the changing political attitude of the host regime. It is for the home office and the finance chief in that office to balance these factors in a score or more of countries against the total performance of the corporation. The manager abroad in one country must remember this when his headquarters refuses capital for expansion or demands remission of profits perhaps not yet earned. Primarily he must re-member that, when he bows to the demand for innumerable reports on the financial status and performance of the sector which he adminis-ters, he is only a part of his company's worldwide pattern.

He is working in an area of tremendous influence on global monetary affairs. Multinational companies produce around 15 per cent of the global world product and their growth is 10 per cent per year, which in thirty years can bring their share of the world product to one-half, making the mammoth firm, of course, a larger target for wary govern-ments and local businesses and a seductive but dangerous partner for needy countries.

Some headquarters are extremely tough in their belief that financial management is the core of their multinational success, and unless they recall that their contribution to the economy of their host countries is part of their excuse for being there, they may be the first to suffer the retribution of governments abroad.

One such financial officer of a home office has plainly set out his views in an article in the *Management Review*, September 1969:

'To be effective, financial control must be applied at the earliest possible moment. The best time to stimulate or restrain action is before it has started . . .

'The second precept of planning as it applies to international operations is that it must be objective. When the planning "points of appraisal" are set realistically, when the premises are understood, and when the period of action still lies in the future, it is possible to get general acceptance on courses of action – even when such programmes have certain aspects that are unpalatable to particular field areas . . .'

It follows naturally, according to this executive, that

'The third precept of international planning is that it must induce action automatically. The plan must point the course and initiate corrective processes as soon as conditions alter . . .

'In a number of cases companies have found it desirable to ensure the objectivity of reporting by establishing a "direct line" reporting relationship between headquarters financial managers and their colleagues within the subsidiaries.'

Translated, this means he would put his own financial man in the subsidiary abroad to undercut the manager by reporting directly to the home office treasurer.

The scope of this financial officer's authority carries a broad definition, for his statement enters the field of overseas monetary change, properly an area of concern for the corporate finance manager.

'The inflation problem must be dealt with in a prompt and positive way. This means that while the early evils of inflation are becoming evident, a corporation must take steps to avoid an insidious decapitalization. Procedures must assure, through price-level corrections, that sales prices are increased to a level concurrent with the increase of all costs.'

In these circumstances, finance controls marketing.

78

A few final declarations show us how to evaluate on the corporate scale the financial director abroad.

'Headquarters must rely on its local director of finance who should be a man of stature and probity. However, to gain further assurance of a full understanding of corporate practices and adherence to its expressed policies, it may also depend upon an internal audit operation . . . The responsibility for accounting performance lies within the local company, but it does not hurt to have a professional second-guesser.'

Stated simply, the home office treasurer is best situated to recommend maximum utilization of the company's funds. He alone has the panoramic view of the company's international operations that will permit judgements as to where funds may most advantageously be found, where tax rates will best permit maintaining liquidity, where interest rates are most favourable and where, other factors being in place, additional investment will provide the best yield. He cannot do all this by himself but his viewpoint provides a wider focus than that in any single country abroad. He, for example, should be able to confront a problem like the following:

The tax rate in country X is 55 per cent. The earnings of the subsidiary in X after taxes is $2 million. The subsidiary needs that amount for new investment. But in countries Y and Z the tax rates are 35 per cent and 38 per cent respectively. At home base the tax rate is 48 per cent. The parent company has plenty of cash reserves on hand. How can it best satisfy the need of the subsidiary in country X? The treasurer decides it will be more advantageous for the parent company to repatriate X subsidiary's $2 million and then send out the equivalent amount in new capital. His reasoning is that at home the tax credit from the $2 million in earnings from country X, being higher, will help offset tax liabilities on earnings from countries Y and Z, where the tax rates are markedly lower than in the home country.

Repatriation and export of new investment will have balanced each other off as regards the home country's balance of payments, but the company will have gained by reducing its total tax liability.

The home office is more objective in establishing means to protect company assets abroad against possible devaluation, through such measures as requiring increases in prices, local borrowing, prompt repatriation of dividends, delays in paying local suppliers, making 'swap' deals, repricing finished goods in inventory, and raising prices of raw materials sent to the subsidiary abroad. The local manager will usually have more sensitivity about local reactions to such policies. He may, on balance and over the long term, be right, but if immediate losses are incurred he may not be present over the long term.

The home office may direct shifts of cash into countries where a revaluation appears probable. This was done in 1971 when the German situation clearly called for revaluation. One result was an outcry against the financial manipulations of multinational companies and the day came closer when international regulations will reduce their options in this area.

Home offices are also better prepared to supervise their firm's overall cash management programmes, using generally the services of banks to reduce 'float time', the period between payment by a customer and the point when the seller can actually use the money. In a series of articles on the uses of cash management, *Business Europe* declares that:

'The trend toward better services in the field of cash management stems from many factors. One obviously is the high cost of money in recent years. Companies have been forced to wring the maximum out of available cash and in the process turned to the banks for help. But a more fundamental impetus has perhaps been the growing sophistication of many international corporate money managers, to whom the intricacies of international banking and banking procedures are no longer a mystery.'[2]

Another article states that:

'In the most narrow sense, international cash management is concerned with the transfer of funds across borders in a manner whereby the corporation maximizes its use of cash. This becomes more complicated when the financial officer considers such factors as:
Investment of short-term cash;
Foreign exchange exposure;
Control procedures;
Relations with the banking network;
Regional and global borrowing needs.'

[2] *Business Europe*, reprint, January 1972.

The deteriorating effect of uncontrolled float time on a company's cash position is shown in the following example:

(The cost of float is the float interval divided by 365 days, multiplied by the annual sales volume.) Assuming that float time averages five days for a company with an annual volume of $100 million and overdraft interest is 8 per cent, then the capital tied up would be $1·37 million and the interest cost would be $110,000. Hence a reduction in float time by one day would lower cash needs by about $275,000 and save roughly $22,000 in interest charges each year.

Business Europe summarizes by pointing out that to money experts

'. . . the general objectives of a satisfactory cash management system should include:

'Reducing float time, not only between the company, its affiliates, and its customers, but also within its banking network: banks will be as inefficient as a corporation permits.

'Ascertaining actual financial costs and how to lower them. Investigating the cost of maintaining compensatory balances to get a prime borrowing rate; of carrying inventory, receivables, and foreign exchange positions; and of banking commissions on foreign and other transactions.

'Optimizing the collection of receipts and disbursement of payments within one country as much as possible. This provides leverage to convince banks to give more favourable treatment.

'Locating multicurrency clearing in usually one operating-and-information centre that can net-out transactions. The treasurer thus will be able to pinpoint trouble spots and take quick action (especially important in this period of floating currency rates). Such a centre also minimizes transit periods, reduces the number of transactions, and produces better quotations on foreign exchange.

'Rationalizing cross-border cash flows by determining which currencies should be used in transactions between different affiliates.'[3]

Add to such goals the desirability of accurately judging when a company's financial exposure abroad should be protected by swaps, switches, forward coverage, and hedging (all somewhat synonymous and all usually involving the exchange for a determined period of hard currency for soft, both to be returned at contracted rates, at interest

[3] *Ibid.*

or premium charges which may or may not be justified by the subsequent exchange-rate changes) and the reasons for centralization of the financial function become more binding. Add, too, the assistance of technology in the centralization process. To the telephone and telex have been added the computer and computer networks, which make centralization easier and more rapid. However, this usually becomes effective only when the data from many different affiliates is reduced to a common financial language and at this point the burden on the office abroad sometimes appears excessive.

The reports demanded from a $50 million affiliate may well be, in fact probably will be, the same as those required of a $2 million office, but the latter will not have the same manpower to churn them out. Regular reporting, not only of the balance sheet and profit and loss, but cash position, inventories and receivables, fixed-asset analyses, a schedule of interdivisional transactions, bank position, prepaid expenses, etc., can be an immense charge upon a small office, leading to the oft heard complaint, 'Why don't they leave me alone to do my job?' The answer, of course, will be: 'This is your job.'

And the response from abroad might well be, 'In that case, why don't they let me have something to say about it? Why are they pricing me out of a chance to show profits and making me sell cheap to Smith over in Brazil?' If the father figure at the home office replies, he will point out that the company's total profit picture will be improved by such a procedure and this is what the business is all about. Hopefully, such an explanation will be remembered at the end of the fiscal year when the losing office's performance is being appraised.

Often the manager abroad is not a financial executive and the corporate treasurer is well aware of this. He is then supplied with or advised to find a good financial officer. If this executive is furnished by the home office some delicacy is called for in establishing lines of reporting. If he enjoys a direct channel to the home office, the local financial officer may overlook his responsibility to the local manager. Cases do exist where the local manager is a national of the affiliate's host country and his financial officer has been sent out by the home office. Such a situation calls for broad understanding on the part of the parties concerned.

Otherwise, the manager abroad may come from the parent company and have hired a local financial officer. This has its advantages and its perils. The local financial man is best suited to act as local controller by virtue of his knowledge of local procedures and regulations. He may, however, have a somewhat provincial attitude which makes it difficult for him to accept local office sacrifices in favour of total corporate goals. He may even take a secret delight in 'putting it over' on the home office by such means as emphasizing that remittances cannot be made or dividends paid, rather than looking for ways to effect the payments. It is then a responsibility of the affiliate manager to be the home office's advocate and bring his local financial man into line. The ideal situation will have a local man in the subsidiary as controller and a home office man on hand as treasurer unless the manager has sufficient financial qualifications to fill that role.

In any of these situations both the company and the local manager lose opportunities for more effective reporting if the manager confines his reports to the forms required. The figures can benefit by local interpretation and informal forecasting. Both at home and abroad it is well to keep in mind the claim of W. Jack Butler and John Dearden that:

'There are more opportunities in companies today to increase overall return on investment through effective management of existing business than through new incremental investment programmes . . . There is no room left overseas for contented companies. Rising economic nationalism and toughening competition are forcing companies to strain harder to stay ahead. The management judgement inherent in balancing international operations can no longer be supported solely by conventional accounting practices – the number of operating variables and alternatives is too great, and the range of management choice is too broad.

'Evaluating the relative performance of affiliates, products, customer groups, and executives around the world is a demanding task. But those companies that succeed in accomplishing this effectively will have within their grasp the opportunity to make better decisions about how to pare their weaknesses and build on their strengths.'[4]

The home office might begin to broaden the flow of pertinent information from subsidiaries abroad by inviting informal interpretations of financial reports. They might implement this specifically by

[4] *Harvard Business Review*, May–June 1965.

setting up at intervals – with the collaboration of local managers – a watch list for each country, a set of specific areas of action where social, economic, and political change can affect the financial status and operations of the company. Possible headings for such a list are Taxes, Inflation, Devaluation and Revaluation, Bank Regulations, Political Climate and Attitudes, Attitudes of Industrial Associations and Labour, Interest Rates, Competitive Practices, Product Life Cycles, and Industry Inventories. For example, one company has listed some of the ways the man on the scene can look for signs of approaching devaluation. Either many of these signs are inaccessible to the home office or the information reaches that centre by ordinary means with considerable delay.

The list includes such admonitions as:

1. Watch the trend in balance of payments. The list cites as an example factors which may escape ordinary notice but which may be crucial to a country's economic health – like tourist income. A sudden falling off of tourism in Spain would be a danger signal.

2. Foreign indebtedness. Usually reported through conventional channels but often related with some delay to the lack of funds to service it.

3. Gold and dollar reserves in a country. Are they pledged against loans and do they include stand-by credits?

4. Negotiations for foreign loans, especially with agencies like the International Monetary Fund. If unsuccessful, why could the country not meet the requirements?

5. Budget deficits. No comment.

6. Crop reports. In a one-crop country a crop failure can mean financial disaster.

7. Suddenly rising prices. Do they mean inflationary pressure?

8. Scarcities and hoarding. Is local business holding goods back for higher prices?

9. Business failures. Are they being caused by attrition of capital and inability to maintain inventories?

10. Real-estate values. Does a boom reflect local fear of inflation?

11. Money in circulation. No comment.

12. Bank credit. Is it tightening as a response to government pressures against inflation?

13. Capital flight. No comment.

The financial representative of a multinational firm who is based in Geneva holds the view that his effectiveness depends largely on how well the home office communicates with him, but acknowledges that the final responsibility for a useful two-way flow of information rests with him.

'I can do my job better when the home office clues me on its plans, projects, and coming requirements. If I know what policy changes are occurring and how they will affect requirements for funding I can start making the proper arrangements before they are asked for.'

Developing the theme, he says,

'The key value of the financial man abroad is as a reporting officer. But not just a routine reporting officer filling out forms. He should be interpreting immediate situations. He should be forecasting the local or regional scene. He should be outlining and interpreting trends. He should be aware of sources of funds and keep the home office advised about them. But the value of his information will be increased in proportion to the home office's advice about its planning.'

Finally, he places the responsibility for the best working relationship on the man abroad.

'It's a matter of communications, of informing and being informed. But you can't count on the home office to handle that. They're too busy. The fellow abroad has to do the pushing and he has to make the communications personal. Reports and the telex won't do. He has to talk to his home office counterparts personally, travel to see them and get them on the phone as often as he can justify. My chairman and his treasurer are in London right now and I haven't heard from them for some days. So I will call them in about an hour and just ask what is going on.

'You have to know how the home office works and keep after them. My parent company is located in a small town, not a world capital. And just like small towners they will get together on Saturday mornings, take their coats off and talk before going out to lunch and maybe golf in the afternoon. Now at those Saturday morning sessions with no chairman, notes or secretaries, a lot of things are decided about how to run the company. And I have a habit of phoning in on some of the sessions just to ask how things are going on and often find out more than a lot of cables or letters would ever tell me.'

He agrees that the manager abroad is a reporter in financial matters, but much more – a prodder, analyst, and interpreter.

The reason, of course, for refusing to assume the routine reporter role is that the manager abroad wants to have some influence on the policies he lives by. He can only accomplish this by injecting his opinion before the company plans are outlined and on this point his ingenuity must find the key to effective communications.

Chapter 6

Who Controls the Market?

The more one penetrates the role of the manager abroad, the more it becomes apparent that it depends on the degree of centralization or decentralization to which his company is committed. However, this apparent simplification conceals complexities within it. As we have seen, even the most decentralized firm tends to hold a firm rein on financial management and as we will observe, the most home-office oriented corporations must concede considerable freedom to the manager afield in the matter of marketing. The qualifications do not end there, because while different industries may share the same viewpoint on finance, their emphasis on marketing varies tremendously. It is not unusual for a man who has made his mark in marketing consumer goods abroad to wind up his career as president of the firm at headquarters, but this is most unlikely when the company is in the petroleum business, heavy industry or banking.

There are two major reasons why the manager abroad holds strong cards in directing the marketing function. One, marketing is an inexact science, loaded with variables and uncertainties. Two, the man in the field is closer to the most important of the variables – the consumer. The home office can claim superior experience and higher calibre marketing specialists, but it has to admit that the changing socio-economic scene is constantly cancelling out the lessons of previous experience and no specialists can safely expound a rigid theory of marketing. As for the all-important relationship with the consumer, the manager abroad is obviously nearer to the action.

The uncertainties of marketing are listed in an extract from an article by Dr Philip Kotler.[1] First on his list is

---

[1] *Coping with the Complexities of Marketing*, Conference Board Record, January 1969.

'Shape of response function. The first major problem is that the shape of the market's response to additional marketing expenditure is typically unknown. If a firm doubles the scale of its marketing expenditures, will its sales double, more than double, or less than double?

'Multiple territories. The second major problem is that the market's response to different levels of marketing expenditure will vary by territory, making it difficult for the firm to determine the best way to allocate its marketing funds. (Obviously, this complexity is compounded for multinational firms.)

'Marketing-mix interaction. The third major problem is that marketing effort, far from being a homogeneous input, is a composite of many different types of activities undertaken by the firm to improve its sales . . . The market's response to variations in the level of any one marketing input is conditional on the level of the other activities . . .

'Delayed response. The fourth major problem is the presence in most companies of more than one product and the consequent need to allocate limited marketing funds among them. Marketing strategies cannot be evolved for each product separately because of the strong demand and cost interactions that generally prevail among different products in the company's line . . .

'Competitive effects. The sixth major problem is that sales results are a function of the relative marketing efforts by the firm and its competitors and the firm has no control over competitors' moves . . .

'Marketing-corporate interactions. The seventh major problem is that marketing decisions cannot be optimized without simultaneous decisions in the production and financial areas . . .

'Multiple objectives. The eighth major problem is that a company tends to pursue multiple and often contradictory objectives.

'Uncertainty effects. The ninth major problem is that the marketing process is full of uncertainties beyond those just isolated . . .'

This ninth major problem could well contain nine more, particularly as the discussion may extend to the international field, where markets vary by peoples, customs, economic scale, and stage of development, as well as ideologies and aspirations. All such considerations become more acute in the international field because firms in that area are more often involved with bringing new products to market; that is, their old products are often new to the market abroad.

An illuminating example of just such a venture was outlined to the Association of National Advertisers in the United States by Mr M. W. Duncan, Vice-President, International Chemicals and Plastics, of the Union Carbide Corporation. The case reaches a successful conclusion but one perceives instances where greater use of the local knowledge of field managers might have accelerated the company's progress and avoided some expensive errors.

Mr Duncan introduced his talk by saying,

'It took five years to complete what we might arbitrarily call the development phase during which our annual exports of SEVIN insecticide grew, in almost geometric progression each year, from one-half million dollars to sixteen million dollars – a period during which we progressed from an unknown to a leading world contender in the field of agricultural chemicals.'

Launching into the story of this marketing exploit, Mr Duncan declared that its success was based on a three-part formula 'consisting of selection, experimentation, and extrapolation'.

The first precept – selection – was, according to Mr Duncan, applied to:

the selection of end-use markets,
the selection of geographical areas,
the selection of distribution methods, and
the selection of business practices.

In selecting its end-use markets the company gave first priority to the cotton-growers because theirs is a large-volume market controlled by few producers, and in many countries they play a vital role as exporters bringing in much-needed foreign exchange. Hence they receive favourable government treatment in financing productive expenditures. Fruit and vegetable growers were given second priority because they are found everywhere and the company had already some domestic experience with them.

The company's selection of geographical areas was broad; Mexico, Central America, and Egypt were the principal cotton-growing targets; Japan, the Philippines and India topped the list for rice production; and parts of Europe, South America, and Africa tagged at the end of the list.

89

Next in the selection phase of the formula was the choice of distribution systems. Here some of the managers abroad were brought into the scheme, for the first choice where possible was to use existing affiliates. Next on the list were exclusive non-affiliated distributors, multiple non-affiliated distributors and distributors in whom the company had made an investment.

Next came the selection of marketing strategies which Mr Duncan called 'business practices', and here the manager in the field had little participation. The home office determined to put prices at a premium because of the special qualities of its SEVIN insecticide. A range of promotion ideas was considered at headquarters, including educational seminars, bringing foreign agricultural experts to the U.S., paying promotion allowances to distributors, going into international trade fairs and, with particular emphasis, producing and exhibiting educational movies to stimulate the interest of distributors and end-users.

An evaluation of the effectivness of these methods is difficult because the impetus toward success was caused by an unforeseen phenomenon – the outbreak of an epidemic of cotton-leaf worm in Egypt. The company was already in the Egyptian market, prepared to respond to the desperate and unexpected need for technical help. It responded with a massive airlift, based on a re-staging of its supply depots and some notably imaginative deployment of the company's and outside resources. The feat won both the Egyptian market and worldwide notice in agricultural circles. Although one wonders whether this stroke of fate did not negate the company's marketing philosophy, Mr Duncan in his exposition cites it as only an aid to the thrust of its efficacy.

He then explained how the second stage, experimentation, operated to fulfil the programme. He recalled the company's experiences in Mexico and the Philippines, where the first distribution strategies failed and experimentation with new formulas solved the problem. However, his exposition overlooked the fact the company already had its own men in those areas and had apparently failed to consult them about local distribution facilities and methods.

The third step in the formula, extrapolation, is a basic attribute of multinational operations. It is simply the transfer to one market of knowledge gained in another. In the case of Mr Duncan's company, it applied in Pakistan lessons learnt in Egypt, but without the benefit of an insect blight, of course. It also introduced in Brazil distribution policies successfully tested in Peru; but Mr Duncan conceded that some adaptation was necessary because of a competitor's surprise counter-attack. In the U.S.S.R., the Egyptian experience proved valuable but the company was wise in adjusting to the special conditions of a state-controlled economy. In fact it did this with some flair, making splendid use of company-sponsored seminars and participation in specialized trade fairs. Although Mr Duncan claimed that the selection – experimentation – extrapolation formula was the key to the company's successful marketing programme, it was in the exceptions to this and the company's ability to adapt quickly to unexpected situations that it emerged most triumphantly.

The case merits study for its illustration of the logical steps followed in an headquarters-developed marketing project. It does not detail the input which field managers contributed, if any, and in its description of mishaps with distribution methods employed in Mexico and Brazil it implies that local advice may have been overlooked or, of course, may have been wrong.

Many variables were eliminated by the nature of the product and its market. A cotton farmer in Egypt and one in Brazil do have the same concerns with regard to insecticides, and when the farmer's crop is at stake the price of the product becomes secondary. However, with variables reduced to a minimum, it was an accident of nature – the threat to Egypt's cotton crop – that accounted for the dynamic start of the five-year project.

At the other end of the international marketing spectrum is the instance of how an American clothing manufacturer, Levi Strauss, brought a novelty product, 'jeans', into favour with the youth market in Australia. Here, locally-obtained knowledge of the market was of the essence; a campaign patterned by the home office would never have coped with the peculiarities of the Australian market, although the home office was alive to its potential. The story is told by *Business Asia* in its June 25, 1971 issue.

'In 1969 the Australian subsidiary of Levi Strauss (LS) set up an import-wholesale house in Sydney to market Levis. The firm knew from the outset that its product had a poor local image. The average Aussie, a conservative fellow, associated jeans with grubby-type people and parents often forbade their daughters to wear them. The fact that locally manufactured jeans were frequently less stylish than Levis, and made of lower quality fabrics, only helped to reinforce the barriers confronting the LS sales force.

'To penetrate this stronghold, the company launched an intensive advertising campaign. LS marketers knew that Australia was a potential gold mine. Because of the mild climate and innumerable beaches, young Australians could wear jeans all year around. And the country's young (i.e. the under twenty-fives) constituted half of the population.

'Using a double-barrelled advertising approach, LS first unleashed an atmospheric pop show tailored to identify Australian youth with the international "Levi set". In this novel presentation, held in a large auditorium, a group of jeans-clad dancers darted on and off stages against a background of pop music, while movie projectors flashed simultaneous films of young people around the world wearing jeans.

'According to LS management, the pop show had phenomenal results, setting the stage for the campaign's second phase, which entailed channelling the firm's advertising theme – "Live Levis" – into print media, radio, and point-of-purchase displays. Posters proclaiming that "Wearing Levis is Better than Wearing Pants" and "Everyone Wears Levis" were distributed. In magazines, colour ads showed that Levis come in all shades – not just blue denim – and that respectable people wear jeans. One ad, for example, carried a "People Get Married in Levis" theme, while another featured a jet-set couple in jeans leaning against their private plane.

'Last year, LS's advertising agency, Jackson Wain & Co. produced a radio commercial against a background of pop music. The commercial caught fire among teenagers who called the radio stations to find out if they could buy the record. This prompted RCA Records to sign a contract with LS to convert the commercial into a record for sale to the public. The record became a hit and sales of Levis to teenagers trebled. Spurred by the success of the RCA record, another pop group has created its version of the "Live Levis" score which will be released shortly as a long-playing record. A 60-second Levis commercial, now running on Australian TV, combines creative photography along with the "Live Levis" soundtrack.

'The results of the campaign have been overwhelming. First, a continual flurry of sales has nearly denuded the LS warehouse, causing a severe stock shortage. Secondly, the demand for Levis has become so acute that Levis shops have sprouted throughout metropolitan areas, and some large retail stores have created separate departments for Levis products . . .'

It would be a convenient simplification to deduce from the two cases cited that non-consumer products are generally marketed internationally under direction from the parent company while consumer products are marketed under strategies devised by the managers abroad. But the exceptions to such a premise are so numerous as to nullify it immediately.

What does appear to emerge from observation of multinational marketing is that some elements of the marketing plan are multinational; that is, formulated for all markets by headquarters, while other elements are structured locally in the separate markets. The application of this concept is nearly as diverse as the companies and products involved, with the elements retained by the parent company differing from company to company. In nearly all cases, however, the idea holds that the parent company determines the global marketing policy and in varying degrees delegates strategy development to the field. The manager in the field must respect the parent company's general approach to marketing, but headquarters usually respects his views on its application in his area.

In most cases, the product and its design originates with the parent company but its adaptation to consumer needs abroad becomes part of the marketing plan. Even as standard a product as Coca-Cola varies in sweetness from country to country according to local tastes. And some General Motors cars, like the Opel, have a design origin outside the home country. Research conducted in the field and interpreted in the field manager's office can lead to such decisions. Certainly cosmetics and hair conditioners stemming from product sources in the United States, Great Britain or France must undergo adaptation in markets where skin textures and colouration are different from those of the source country. Branded and processed foods must meet local tastes. Pharmaceutical products must adhere to local laws and local traditions. When the parent company can avoid these changes of product formula or design, as in the case of cigarettes and liquors, it achieves some economies of production and can better serve the tourists

93

and business travellers who seek products with which they are already familiar.

There are also occasions when multinational companies may decide to create foreign markets for their products, on the basis that if a product or product concept has succeeded in one market, other markets may be persuaded to accept it. Quaker Oats did this in Argentina when it applied the idea of quickly cooked oats to a traditional local food, a type of corn meal called polenta. Polenta is part of the tradition of Spanish cooking and housewives had long accepted the necessity to cook it for hours to prepare it for the table. The Quaker company found a way to process polenta so that it could be cooked in minutes and decided to package its product for Argentine use. Many advisers warned that housewives would reject the new product, viewing it with suspicion and resenting its takeover of their attributes as cooks. Quaker's local management counselled otherwise. It was aware that, priced higher than the traditional polenta, the Quaker product would meet resistance from the low-income group, but it also knew that most of the middle and upper classes employed servants who would welcome being freed from hours spent over the stove, so the marketing programme was designed to introduce Quaker Instant Polenta into Argentine homes through their servants. The effort was successful.

Pricing is another element of the marketing plan that the parent company and the local management abroad share. Popular products like Pepsi and Coca-Cola are priced in their countries of origin with the idea that they must be made available to everyone. In countries with such a low level of income that large sectors of the population are out of the market for most products, this becomes impossible. There these soft drinks, rather than being simply convenient means of providing refreshment, take on an atmosphere of prestige, of being the fashionable adjunct to gatherings of the young and the would-be young. Manufacturers of cigarettes and popular drugs like analgesics meet the problem of poor economies with different solutions. They allow retailers to open packages and sell cigarettes in units of one, two, or three or more. And the analgesic makers, in many parts of Latin America and the Pacific-Orient, package their tablets in envelopes containing one, two, or three, and sell them in such unorthodox outlets as newspaper kiosks and bars. It then becomes incumbent on the local manager, whose advice on pricing and packaging has been followed, to find the merchandising and promotional approaches which reach the markets and the situations for which the product style has been adapted. In Brazil, where the annual carnival is certain to give most of the population a headache at some time during the celebration, a resourceful local manager asked his advertising staff to commission a samba with a carnival rhythm but words extolling the company's analgesic. The company then maintained the popularity of the tune for the rest of the year with generous infusions of paid radio spots.

Not all products have the elasticity to meet economic differentials with repackaging or shifts of promotional strategy. In a poorer economy, television sets and electric shavers remain accessible to a favoured few and the producer can do little about it but keep his prices up. Again, there are exceptions and the British market became one when television sets could be placed in British homes by renting rather than outright sale. However, this could be done because the economy was structured with the financial backing for hire-lease promotion.

Distribution is another phase of marketing where the guidance of the manager abroad is essential. His home office can hardly appreciate the importance of kiosks in many European countries, or of the vans that career through the Philippine countryside as the only means of bringing popular products to the largest sector of the market. Only in the locality can one obtain an appreciation of the distribution systems in Switzerland, where a food packager soon finds he must opt for one of two or three major chain outlets or take his product to the small stores, which usually excludes it from the chain stores.

Distribution patterns require continuous local surveillance because in most markets abroad they change rapidly and continuously. The local manager in the field can rarely rest on a single recommended strategy. He is surrounded by change and must constantly revise his forecastings. To the extent possible, he is also busy keeping his company flexible enough to move with the market. Distribution of food and other popular-priced consumer products has undergone a revolution with the advent of supermarkets, chain stores, and the association of independent stores into buying units. Meanwhile, small retail units have been vanishing. The figures for the U.K. are dramatic: 285,000 retail food outlets in 1950, shrinking to 217,000 in 1967, and forecast to diminish to 135,000 in 1977. In specialized shops, such as butchers, bakers, fruit stores etc., the change is even more notable. There were 140,000 of these shops open in 1950, 100,000 reported to be in operation in 1969, and the estimate for 1977 is 55,000.

Concurrently, the number of buying points which must be contacted by the marketer has shrunk and the influence of wholesalers who reach these points is increasing. Local management must not only shift its manner of reaching the consumer market; it must also recast its sales staff and their mode of operation. The series of moves by Heinz, a U.K. market leader, is a case in point. Heinz products are stocked in nearly all food retail outlets, but not by the same methods as a decade ago when Heinz ceased to make direct calls on most of these outlets and increased its sales pressure on wholesalers and the large buying groups. Over a three-year period, Heinz increased its sales through wholesalers from 10 per cent to 40 per cent of its volume. Other companies, such as Beechams, Kraft, and Nestlé, also shifted their marketing patterns in a similar manner.

Markets change. So do companies, by growing and adapting their marketing strategies to their new potential. The changes will often occur in the field according to recommendations from the management abroad. There is the case of the company manufacturing scientific instruments and measuring devices. These products are for highly sophisticated buyers who require a high level of sales counsel and service. As this company spread branches throughout Europe, it found it necessary to withdraw from sales agencies and recruit its own highly trained sales staff.

Another company markets labelling machines to three different sectors of the European market: industrial, commercial, and domestic consumer. To sell the same product to these three groups of buyers it divides its distribution between exclusive distributors for the industrial and commercial markets, and wholesalers for the general retail market. Its locally recommended innovation is to appoint a marketing advisor for each country, a national of the country who has trained for two years at headquarters.

Multinational marketing circles continue their controversy over the merits of the global advertising campaign versus those of the campaign designed independently for each foreign market. One wonders whether the discussion is kept alive primarily to fill the pages of trade magazines, because certain principles are irrefutably emerging. Perhaps they can be indicated by looking at products and packages. It is obvious that a multinational marketer wants to maintain control over product policy and quality. However, he will yield when necessity requires, as in the cases we have mentioned of cosmetics, foods, and even automobile models. He will also concede to the demands of local markets in matters of packaging, and there is usually close collaboration between the manager abroad and the home office experts in finding compromises between the home market package and the one which will be presented to the foreign market. There is no controversy on these points. In a sense the product is the company's policy and the package is its advertisement. Shifting directly to the advertising function, the parent company seeks to establish policy, and the field office takes the lead in strategy.

One may attempt to refute the proposition by citing such consistently patterned global advertising as Coca-Cola's. Coca-Cola provides advertising guidance to its bottlers around the world, rather firm guidance, in fact. It supplies bottlers annually with a pattern book containing advertisements, scripts for radio and TV commercials, poster designs, and designs for point of sale. The theme for the campaign is suggested. A bottler may demur, but he must persuade the company that he has good reason for doing so. Many do. But nuances of a Coca-Cola campaign differ from market to market, in accordance with local language, customs, economies, and media availabilities.

An apparently simple theme like 'It's the Real Thing' can assume different meanings with changing social conditions and shifts in language. First launched in the United States, 'It's the Real Thing' contained a double-pronged attack. By innuendo it implied that the major competing product was – well, not quite genuine. It also spoke the rebellious language of the young who are in open revolution against sham in every form and who are almost religious in their search for the non-synthetic. But as the campaign travels it can assume new shapes. In a country suffering from a lack of drinkable water supply, 'It's the Real Thing' speaks for Coke's purity of ingredients. In a society where Coca-Cola's price leaves the mass behind, and it does in some, 'It's the Real Thing' implies fashionable approval and declares that the product is worth the price for those who can pay it.

The Esso Tiger campaign of some years ago is usually cited by defenders of global, as against national, advertising. The example is a good one – for both sides of the argument. The campaign was a sensational success in its first and second years. It had all the advantages claimed for multinational advertising. It had been developed by top creative people in Esso's international advertising agency, McCann-Erickson. Artwork, films and basic design were produced at a central point with copies for the field, saving vast sums in the advertising production budget. The campaign was recognizable wherever travelling motorists might be, adding spill-over weight to the campaign. Spill-over is the bonus audience of a magazine sold outside its own country, or the cross-border listeners to radio or TV stations. Esso had a campaign which allowed it to exercise home office control. Finally, the gentle but muscular Tiger held an umbrella over nearly all Esso world-wide promotional efforts.

But unwanted visitors crept under the umbrella and managers in the field began to protest. Competitors attacked with expansive give-away promotions and contests with expensive prizes. Much as the public loved the Tiger, it showed signs of loving cash – or other – prizes more. And where this occurred field affiliates were loud in their protests to the home office. In Germany, the Tiger's association with motor power began to sound like encouragement for speedier motoring at a time when the holocaust on German highways was arousing alarm, especially amongst the authorities. In other countries, Esso was in danger of being known as the Tiger Company and the parent company grew new wrinkles on its forehead. Elsewhere, pinpoint promotional needs could not be met with an umbrella campaign and sub-campaigns, locally-oriented, began to appear.

After an agonizing, and unsuccessful, search for another global theme, the Tiger was quietly retired. Country affiliates again began to meet their promotional needs with campaigns tailored to suit their separate environments. In Europe, where motorists cross borders more often than elsewhere, a regional umbrella campaign, based on 'The New Europeans', was launched as an adjunct, but not a substitute, for local country campaigns.

Other international advertisers who have had to make local exceptions in their advertising are cited in 'Advertising Takes Off', by Shelley Wanger.[2]

---

[2] *Vision*, February 1972.

'For one thing, the state of the market and of the competition can vary immensely from one country to another. To demonstrate this side of the argument, Doyle Dane Bernbach remarks that it was not until British car prices rose at one point that Volkswagens, which the agency handles, could be sold in Britain with their continental image of high quality at low cost.'

Other examples are:

'Only a small number of Frenchmen fly each year, so Pan Am has kept its slogan, "The World's Most Experienced Airline", in France. Elsewhere it has been dropped because it has become less effective as air travel has become more familiar.

'In Britain or France most clients of Evinrude outboard motors will be buying their first outboard and for them the outboard is essentially connected with water sports. In Scandinavia this is more a replacement market: buyers may be on their second or third motor. It is also a market in which the outboard is widely used for fishing and transport.'

Because of exceptions raised on both sides, the dispute continues. Manufacturers of industrial and other capital goods, makers of expensive watches, banks and car rental firms, speak for the advantages of international advertising.

Perhaps the problem rests in the tendency to think of advertising apart from marketing, the inclination to forget that it is essentially a spokesman for the marketing programme. Once a balanced view has been restored, it is easier to approach the principle that the parent company states marketing policy and is well advised to let its subsidiaries propose strategies that conform to it and to their local circumstances.

Parent companies – and the affiliates afield – will do well to keep three precepts in mind in carrying out this division of responsibility. One, surveys on new product failures usually list as the first cause for collapse the lack of sufficient preparatory market research. This is even more true in the strange environment of foreign markets than the familiar one of domestic operations. Since a large proportion of products and services introduced abroad by multinational firms are new to the foreign markets, such research is required even for products which have passed the test of the domestic crucible. Co-ordinated action of home office experts and the manager abroad in setting up visible studies of the local foreign market before an investment is made in product or service introduction would appear to be an elementary, if often overlooked, preliminary step.

A corollary to the above proposition calls for a review of the product's place in its life cycle at home and its probable place in the field. Because a product has reached maturity in the headquarters market, or may even be on the decline, that is no assurance that it is not going to be at the start of the curve in the foreign market. Polaroid's experience in France is a case in point. The company skipped the educational phase of its merchandising in France on the assumption that the product was understood there as well as it was in the United States. Time and money were lost in correcting the marketing and advertising strategy. The Evinrude outboard-motor example also makes the point. New on the product life cycle in Britain and France, outboard motors are in the mature stage in Scandinavia.

Finally, it is becoming increasingly apparent that the marketing concept must be sold as well as the product. In some cases the marketing concept *is* the product. The success of Avon cosmetics rests not upon the magic of product formulas but upon the innovatory distribution system of house-to-house saleswomen who can speak to prospective buyers in their own language, in their own home surroundings and, by appointment, when the prospect is ready to set aside her housework and enjoy an interesting chat with a nice young woman.

Coca-Cola's marketing plan is sold to its bottlers with the same vigour that it applies to advertising to the public. Only the bottler who has learnt how to distribute Coca-Cola can be a successful part of the marketing plan. Holiday Inns' success is based on a marketing plan which designs and locates the product to reach its target market. Then the franchised proprietor learns to offer a type of service that will satisfy the market. IBM's close control of its sales centres focuses on expert personal counsel and service which are an essential part of IBM's marketing plan. And IBM's advertising usually emphasizes the point by implication, and not so directly as to risk offence.

In the adherence to these principles the manager abroad is a key figure. Should he become disheartened about the limitations placed upon him in the financial management of his assignment, let him look to marketing for an outlet. The sternest of parent organizations will welcome his fullest co-operation, his soundest advice and his most imaginative proposals in developing and executing the plans that bring the product and the buyer together.

Chapter 7

Labour Pains and Issues

In allocating responsibility for the different functions of management, parent companies are usually content to assign personnel matters and labour relations to their managers abroad who, for their part, are satisfied to accept the charge. The exception occurs at management and submanagement levels. Here the home office claims authority regarding terms of employment and it reserves the final word on employing men who may eventually aspire to replace the field manager.

Only recently has this noncontroversial arrangement been challenged, albeit inadvertently, and the paradox is that the challenge comes from the ranks of labour itself. The thrust of unions towards international confrontation with multinational companies may well soon return responsibility for industrial relations to the home office. Centralization will then be injected into international business where it is least wanted. The movement is under way. Some years may pass before it reaches its climax and when it does there may be a new alignment of interests between multinational management, labour, and the nation state. Host governments already suffer some discomfort in harbouring the growing power of multinational corporations. When these firms are accompanied by multinational labour organizations, or when governments see their domestic labour unions responding to directives from abroad, they may become even more disconcerted. Indeed, in those nations whose labour unions are categorized as political entities, the international labour movement may be seen as an intolerable invasion of sovereignty. It is not inconceivable that government reactions may well come down on the side of the multinational corporations, at least on this issue, or they may join with local labour against both the multinational firms and the international labour organizations that pursue them. At present the challenge is incipient but there are enough solid instances of international labour action to require that in this area, as in others, the field manager observe and report the situation carefully.

Meanwhile, the manager abroad is still pretty much master in his own house in matters concerning his workforce. The exceptions to this statement usually act to reinforce its validity. Two notable cases are those of American companies who gave orders to their managers in France to shut down their plants with all possible haste. The dismissal on immediate notice of hundreds of workers infuriated French authorities, whose policies include a concern for employment which they expect employers to share. Furthermore, they expect employers to assume the costs of shifting labour when it is made redundant. Finally, they abide by the unwritten expectation that the government will be consulted regarding any plans which include serious cutbacks in employment. In the cases cited, local management was forced to accept orders from home. There are other occasions, too, when local management must accept a bitter pill from the parent company and ask its workforce to share it. This will occur when a local branch has been doing its job well but because the parent company's books reflect a poor worldwide picture it is asked to defer bonuses or salary increases in order to supply funds to the parent company. Fortunately, the reactions to such decisions are teaching home offices to avoid such directives when possible.

As to the working policies that determine a manager's relationship with his employees, these are usually left to his own determination, if only because by proximity he is best qualified to make the necessary judgements. But proximity alone is hardly enough to sustain the local field manager. Assuming he possesses the sensitivity, adaptability and good judgement to be effective, he will have to add a knowledge of the local social values to his arsenal, or find competent local advisors on whom he can depend. Some of these values have been analysed and listed, and certainly their application to different countries, even those in the same region, are as diverse as the deepest roots of national cultures.

The history of a country carries implications, if not explanations, of how its people will react to modern management and particularly to management imported from abroad. Is a country's history a story of violence, of tribal warfare, of struggle against repression? Is it a

103

saga of independence, perhaps of aggression? Is national pride a motivating force and if so, is it rooted in intellectual accomplishment or adherence to indigenous religion, or does it stem from the leadership of dictatorial heroes? Are the people emerging from colonialism wary, sensitive, and quick to protect all aspects of their new-found sovereignty? Of the traditions which have survived, which form the core of the contemporary social environment and which are susceptible to modification? How does the residue of history influence the country's present aspirations? What part of its society shares them?

The questions of history are of course innumerable, and their translation into contemporary terms directly affects management styles. Where, for instance, does the family stand in society? In Japan the authority of the head of the family is still unchallenged and the Japanese employee expects to find a father figure at the head of his company. In India the family is subject to opinions from all its members, and the Indian employee expects to encounter no surprise when he offers his suggestions on management policy. In France the family stays in its birthplace for generations, and moving a French employee from one part of the country to another is almost unthinkable. In America families themselves are out of fashion and employees at all levels change their place of residence almost as easily as their shirts.

As a framework for study of the local culture a checklist, to be reviewed, revised, and rearranged as knowledge is accumulated, can be a useful tool for the manager abroad. He might list the vital factors thus:

1. *Satisfaction – or aspiration.* Is the society competitive and if so, at all levels? Or does it place security above ambition? Perhaps ambition is only for those who are favoured to enter religious, intellectual, and political pursuits, while commerce still shares the status of street traders. Or perhaps money can buy status and working ambition can be easily instilled.

2. *Nepotism.* In many Western countries whose management principles are firmly rooted in a striving for efficiency, nepotism is suspect and usually rejected, except for some family-owned companies with diminishing influence. In other societies accustomed to the dominance of family-owned enterprise or where business morality is such that it

engenders suspicion of the stranger, nepotism is accepted, even approved, as good policy.

3. *Group and personal loyalties.* This includes the importance of the family as well as the tribal, ethnic, and political background of the society. One should also measure the ability of the individual to stand alone on specific issues, and the value of man-to-man relationships which affect the degree to which an employer-employee relationship can or should be personalized. And one would be alert to the possibility of ethnic, religious or other group splits within the company's work-force.

4. *Attitudes toward authority and responsibility.* The evaluation would take into account the degree of deference to authority, the conditioning to certain types of authoritarian control, and whether or not these reactions carry a willingness to accept responsibility.

5. *Educational and intellectual background.* A knowledge of how training will be received by employees and whether it must be under-taken by rote or motivation can make the manager aware of oppor-tunities and pitfalls. It can also inform him about the acceptability of new methods and concepts to the upper levels of his personnel.

6. *Status and prestige.* These important points can indicate the key to motivation and signal the areas which require careful handling. In some societies, a uniform, especially that of a plant supervisor, can mean a great deal more than changes in wages. In others, it is the difference between skilled and unskilled workers which has a social significance. In all, and at nearly all levels, the idea of self-respect has varied meanings and each of them goes deep. In many Latin American countries the *amor proprio* of every man is carefully guarded, some-times violently. This 'self-love' is a sort of enhanced self-respect and its expressions and its vulnerabilities can only be ignored with some recklessness. Compounding the problem is the diversity of the *amor proprio* concept, for its application by a banker is far distant from that of a welder. Until it is understood, humour in personal relationships is perilous. The kidding or bantering of the Anglo-Saxon can encounter a fierce reaction in a Latin whose *amor proprio* has been wounded. More

important, a refined sensitivity to the sense of self-respect of the Latin can win his undying loyalty and stimulate his efforts to be helpful with no thought of personal gain.

As the manager absorbs his environment this list will grow, and it is an enriching if sometimes maddening experience to enlarge it. But wherever it ends or begins, the host nation's organization of labour relations and the customs supporting it must take a pre-eminent place. Although the structure of obligations shared by employers and plant workers has no formal relationship to the attitudes of office workers, it does reflect a nation's views on labour and so it affects the point of view of the white-collar employee. In the United States, where a guaranteed annual wage is often a disputed issue, the executive and semi-executive class tend toward contractual employment. In Japan, where company unions are the norm, office workers see themselves as permanent adjuncts of the company. In the countries of Europe where the workers seek participation in management their elders in offices share the goal. The variations on the theme are as numerous as the nations that may house the subsidiaries of a multinational company, and in each case the field manager must make his adjustments. On a quick world tour one encounters:

Israel, where 90 per cent of labour is unionized and where the unions are federated under Histadrut, a powerful organization whose voice is heard in politics and whose central organization enters into nearly all union bargaining. Histadrut also controls one-sixth of Israel's industry.

Egypt, where the government holds control over the unions. If either the employer or the union involved in a dispute requests government arbitration, it becomes compulsory. In this climate strikes are rare.

India. Where labour is organized, it coalesces into small and weak company unions. There is bargaining on wages and work conditions but fringe benefits, in general, are set by the government.

Japan. There are 50,000 company unions joined in four federations which have political overtones. Since employment is a lifetime obligation and wages are raised according to length of service, there is little open controversy. Employers establish fringe benefits on a paternalistic basis and they are often impressively generous, including workers' clubs, education allowances for children, and encouragement to workers to join in cultural pursuits.

The *Philippines* share the oriental trend towards weak labour organizations, with 2,800 company unions bargaining separately with their employers and neither side having the government as a partner, although in a crunch the employer is more likely to be favoured.

In *Singapore* the hand of the government is strong in labour arrangements. As an anti-inflation measure, the government tends to repress wage increases for unskilled workers but as an antidote it manages worker training programmes and encourages profit-sharing.

In *Belgium* the workers organize independently but exert strong influence on their government, which assumes responsibility for employment. The effect on the white-collar class is remarkable, with regulations requiring a three-month dismissal period for salaried employees up to their ninth month of employment, while higher-salaried men and women are promised more on negotiated contracts.

In *France* labour unions are highly political and shun offers of participation in management for fear of losing the militant loyalty of their men. By law workers' committees have the right to sit in on board meetings as observers, but employers usually avoid this by holding their meetings unannounced and off the premises. Legally imposed fringe benefits range between 55 per cent and 60 per cent of wages. Profit-sharing is required when firms employ a workforce of over one hundred and earn over 5 per cent of their net worth. Profit-sharing takes different forms, accepted by both parties, ranging from distribution of company shares, deposits in a mutual fund, accumulation in a loan to the company, to outright cash payments.

In *Germany* the concept of worker participation in management has reached its most advanced position in the Western world and seems to have smoothed rather than hampered harmonious employer-labour relations. The structure has evolved from decisions of the postwar allied occupation forces, particularly in dealing with the coal, iron and steel industries.

At present there are sixteen strong unions in Germany, and the metal workers' group is the largest in the world. Laws require all corporations employing more than five hundred people to allow one-third employee representation on their supervisory boards, two of whom must be company employees. The remainder are usually union officials. The supervisory board names the managing board and appoints its chairman. The managing board runs the company but it must report periodically on its performance to the supervisory board.

All companies with over five employees must accept works councils whose members are elected by the employees. The council shares in management decisions on all matters directly affecting the workers, except compensation. Companies of over one hundred employees must also have an economic committee which acts as bridge between the works council and management. The system resolves itself into a continuous bargaining process which avoids most crises and strikes.

In the iron, coal and steel industries, the employees have achieved parity on the supervisory boards which include one neutral member to break deadlocks. Here the managing board also includes a labour director in charge of personnel matters. The goal of all German unions is to achieve the privileged state of the unions in the iron, coal, and steel industries.

In *Spain* a manager finds he is engaged with government-controlled unions with no legal right to strike. Government arbitration ends all disputes and the government reviews all agreements for adherence to its economic plan. Regardless, wages have been rising at a rate of 15 per cent per year.

In *Argentina* the unions, on the other hand, at one time appeared to control the government. They were brought together under a single federation during the regime of the dictator Juan Peron and they have never since lost their power and unity. The remaining Peronista party is centred in the Confederacion General de Trabajo which delivers the largest bloc vote in any election which may occur. For this reason recent military governments have avoided elections. A manager confronting this union is facing the militant mass, resentful of post-Peron governments and still seething with a xenophobic bitterness instilled by Peron.

In *Brazil* labour organizations are weak, with only about 10 per cent membership. To protect the workers, laws require prompt arbitration of disputes. Authorized fringe benefits account for about 60 per cent of payrolls. They include such showcase grants as handsome leisure clubs, allowances for child education and spectacles for workers and their families, as well as dental care and generous maternity benefits.

In *Mexico* the labour organizations are not strong but with the help

108

of a sympathetic government they can so complicate matters for a foreign company that most international firms, and many national ones, employ a local labour supervisor to conduct continuous negotiations.

In *Sweden* the tripartite collaboration of industry, labour and government is well known. It will soon take on new manifestations which we shall discuss. Meanwhile it is interesting to observe that Swedish labour tends to lend a helping hand to its counterparts in other Nordic countries when they seem to need support.

None of the situations described above or those in other countries are frozen. They require the attention of the local manager but they put a tax on his alertness because they are in flux as the forces of industry, labour and government gain or lose in the positions they hold. A dramatic example is the change in labour laws in Pakistan after that country's catastrophic war with India and Bangladesh. Workers went on the streets to claim major wage increases and the government issued a series of decrees which sent them back to the factories with many other concessions instead. Now factory workers are allowed to elect 20 per cent of the plant directors. They also have the right to have their own auditor check the company's financial records and to authenticate their share of 4 per cent of a firm's profits and 10 per cent of any increased profits caused by greater productivity. They can elect their own shop stewards by secret ballot, but disputes will be adjudicated by a labour court. Strikes can be voted in secret ballot. The workers are now relieved of paying 2 per cent of wages towards social security, while employers have raised their share from 4 per cent to 6 per cent. Employers are also required to pay for the education of one child in each worker's family and they are expected to pay 5 per cent of the payroll into a workers' housing fund.

More gradual but equally threatening to employers is the development of plant-occupation tactics in the U.K. and Italy. Dramatized in the Upper Clyde shipyards, the movement started some years earlier than the incident there. The call for occupation of factories went out when the fusion of British General Electric, English Electric, and AEI was followed by the closure of several factories. Union dissension saved the company at that time, in 1968. Plessey encountered a similar reaction when it attempted to move its equipment from one plant in Alexandria, Scotland, to another in Ilford, England. A solution was

109

reached only when Plessey found a buyer for the Alexandria plant who promised to turn it into an industrial estate which would absorb the redundant workers. When Thorn attempted to close its factory in Liverpool, workers occupied the plant and in four weeks exacted an agreement to keep the facility going for at least two more years. The British Steel Corporation and Alfred Herbert, machine tools, later backed away from plans to close factories when they were threatened with similar counteraction.

In Italy in January 1972, ten plants were occupied in the province of Rome. Coca-Cola's ARIB bottler had been occupied for over 150 days and the Pantenella food processing plant had been taken over by workers eight months previously. Cartière Tiburtine, acquired by United Paper Mills of Finland, had been occupied for more than six months to block a liquidation sale.

Changes in the worldwide labour scene flare up unexpectedly and separately, like brush fires in a vast dry field in autumn. While some challenge employer power, others promise added strength to management. Northern Europe and Scandinavia are the leading innovators in the field of labour relations.

Swedish labour, nationally on a par with industry and the government in labour negotiations, has emphasized its works councils and planning of plant conditions. Recently it moved toward the German position in demanding a place on company boards. A law acceding to this request went into effect at the start of 1973. It will give Swedish labour one-third of the places on the boards of all companies with fifty or more employees. Interestingly, the law will probably also go into force in Denmark, Norway, and Finland.

In fact Norwegian management is making preparations for greater employee participation in the conduct of company business. An example is the decision of Norsk Teknisk Porselen of Frederikstad to organize a management training project under the direction of the Norwegian Productivity Institute and Industrikonsulent, a management consultancy.

The plan calls for outlining four prime areas of concern, then grouping study teams under each heading. The subject areas are: the organization and its workings, work preparation and planning, waste problems, and product development and marketing. Groups limited to five men undertake studies of each topic. Each group includes two plant workers, a foreman, a member of management, and an R & D representative. The chairman of each group cannot rank higher than the foreman. Periodic meetings lead to the presentation of ideas to top management.

Benefits to date have been specific. The opportunity for workers to discuss management problems in an informal atmosphere has led to their greater appreciation of management concerns. The process has acted as a training course for worker representatives who will in future be involved in legalized worker-participation procedures. Some group suggestions have led to solutions of immediate problems. The group attacking waste problems has found ways of cutting 80 per cent of losses per year.

Nearby, a Swedish company has tackled a problem which produced laughs nearly half a century ago when Charlie Chaplin starred in *Modern Times* and which has always been a burden on assembly workers and psychologists concerned with their mental health: the dehumanizing effects of the assembly-line system.

Volvo, Sweden's largest car manufacturer, has been experimenting with methods to disengage its workers from the grip of the assembly line, seeking solutions through self-governing groups, job rotation, job enlargement, or a combination of the three. The self-governing groups include three to seven men at stations on the line who elect their own leaders and, paid collectively, share earnings. A new man on the team is apprenticed according to team rules and finance.

Job rotation is practised by some seven hundred workers in the plant, each of whom learns through this system the work of all the others in his group. It calls for job changes according to a fixed schedule. Those workers preferring to stay with the same job are allowed to do so.

Job enlargement allows a worker to combine two or more elements of the work on the assembly line.

The goal is to improve interpersonal relationships in the shop and make the work more meaningful for the workers. Management also gains by training a more versatile workforce able to fill in where absenteeism and sickness cut into the regular force.

Workers' councils, feared by many employers, are proving their value in Holland. When first established by law in 1970, or rather when the old law was made effective, the prerogative accorded the councils

111

seemed challenging indeed. They were to have the right to joint decisions on salary payments, training, promotion, job evaluation, and hiring and dismissal policies. They were to be consulted on proposed mergers, expansions, or shutdowns. They were to be allowed to present outside consultants to management meetings. They were entitled to discuss the annual report with management and to be informed in advance in the case of the replacement of a general manager.

Legally the councils were established in 1950 but with no power. Few companies availed themselves of their potential or allowed their voices to be heard. One which did not was Thomassen & Drijver-Verblifa of Deventer, which in 1969 decided to close down one of its plants without consulting its workers. It offered to move the plant's workforce to another neighbourhood and, following demonstrations, to pay all moving expenses. A works council existed, but the company avoided consultation with it. Finally, after the issue reached Parliament, discussions were opened. Eight workers offered to take over the condemned plant and manage it themselves on a co-operative basis. The men were experienced and willing to invest their own cash, and the company viewed the proposal with sympathy. The solution promised to keep the plant open and maintain workers in their jobs. It also allowed management to free itself of its obligation.

The works-council concept has since developed in Holland and in 1972 it became obligatory for any company with over one hundred workers to set up such a council. The management of most companies has accepted the idea while understanding that the Dutch works' councils will have more power than the codetermination systems established in nearby countries. Industry organizations are operating training programmes to prepare workers to fulfil their obligations on the councils. The larger firms have observed that the election of representatives to their works councils are conducted with all the verve of municipal elections, making some of them the largest electoral exercises outside of the parliamentary ones.

International companies have already found new values in the relationship with workers that the works councils encourage. Gulf Nederland N.V. finds no problems either with its council or with the qualifications of its members. IBM Nederland, more accustomed to direction from central offices, had more difficulty adjusting to the new requirement but did so by setting up training programmes to give

112

council members a better understanding of the company's management philosophy and practices.

Other companies have gone much further in making consultants rather than adversaries of their works councils. The Royal Dutch Steelworks postponed its decision to merge with the German Hoesch steelworks until the deal was fully explored with its works council. The company also includes on its agenda for works council meetings such subjects as production problems, foreign worker recruitment, technical training, plant closures, new wage systems, changes in working hours, new investment plans and guaranteed housing loans.

The DAF motor company is one of the more enthusiastic supporters of the works council system. Its retiring co-founder has stated that:

'We have found that the works council is necessary to enable the management and representatives of the personnel to exchange ideas. An industrialist must not only be able to make a quick decision when a commercial problem pops up but must react even more promptly when the interests of his employees are at stake. That is why regular contact between management and staff representatives is of vital importance. In this connection I may mention that in all the forty-three years of DAF's existence there has never been any industrial conflict of any note.'

Another company which had not yet learned the lessons of DAF and was still troubled by its works council reached an agreement that two outside experts should be invited to give short courses to the council members on reading a balance sheet and the principles of management. The courses were popular and were repeated. The reported results have been: higher productivity because of greater worker interest in company goals, a better negotiating atmosphere, and useful proposals from the council as to the solution of internal problems.

The works-council plan apparently offers certain benefits to the subsidiary manager abroad. It can provide him with a group of in-company consultants who understand the business and, more important, the background and developments in labour relations in the host country. In some cases, of course, the recommendations and demands of the council may point to decisions unpalatable to the parent company and put the manager in the position of odd man out. And if he is an American manager, he may find it difficult to reconcile himself

113

to the delays and compromises imposed by the works-council system. On the other hand, a friendly relationship with the company works council can strengthen the manager's hand in dealing with the home office and with the local authorities.

On balance, multinational companies tend to be more generous with their workforces than national companies in terms of wages and working conditions, but not always in establishing the important fringe benefits such as employee clubs and family aid. This has not always protected them from union action or official disapproval – as Ford discovered in England when it incurred wage disparities between regions, and as companies have found in France when their higher wages tended to upset the government's control over the national economic plan.

Probably the greatest point of vulnerability of the multinational corporation is its power, its potential for disruption of labour standards, and its ability, through the diversion of work schedules, to walk away from pressure at one point by moving production to another. There is little tendency to use or abuse this power, for to do so is expensive and distracting. But the power is there and labour leaders with an international viewpoint have decided to organize against it. In so doing, they may be aware of opportunities to increase their own power. The American AFL-CIO has taken more than a neighbourly interest in the cause of labour in Latin America over some decades, claiming to have provided training for 60,000 active trade unionists in the Latin-American countries as well as having sponsored workers' banks, low-cost housing, community and self-help projects and service centres for agricultural workers and small farmers. Employers have not viewed such activity with an unkindly eye, as they have approved the resultant formalization of the union system and the inculcation of a greater sense of responsibility in contract negotiations.

The more aggressive wing of the international labour movement, however, is based in Europe in headquarters that has given rise to the term 'permanent world council', and which aims to insert the works council idea into Common Market regulations dealing with the European company. Development of international labours' ambitions will surely have an impact on the headquarters of multinational companies, while reducing the independence of the field manager to deal with labour relations in his area. This tendency may have its limits, however, because at some point it may also cut into the power of the local labour unions to deal directly with company subsidiaries in their countries, as they do now.

To date some specific steps have been taken in the direction of international labour co-ordination and although they have been encouraging to its proponents they have not yet caused major problems for international business. Charles Levinson, secretary-general of the International Federation of Chemical and General Workers' Union (ICF), reported some of these moves in a paper for an OECD seminar:

'It has become almost routine in branches of our industry which are highly multinationalized such as glass, rubber, and paper, for a parent union to intervene with the parent management on behalf of a union in dispute with a subsidiary – particularly with subsidiaries in less-developed countries.

'By way of examples, such measures have been taken in regard to a Union Carbide strike in the United States; a dispute with the Scripto Pen Company in Atlanta, Georgia; Cyanamide in New Jersey; American Goodyear and Firestone rubber companies in Germany, Turkey and Malaya; Italian Pirelli Company in Italy, Turkey and Brazil; the German Bayer Company in the United States; the Australian United Asbestos Company in the Fiji Islands; Libby-Owens-Ford plant in Germany; National Fertilizer Company in Morocco; Swedish Belleruid Paper Company in Portugal; French Michelin rubber company in Spain.'

Continuing his report, Mr Levinson said:

'Another approach is through negotiation between ICF headquarters and top management of the parent company. Such intervention helped win a three-month strike of a Japanese chemical union a short time ago against the subsidiary of the Geneva-based, worldwide General Superintendence Company. When the workers of a Turkish subsidiary of the giant German chemical company, Hoechst, were forced to go on strike, the ICF entered the dispute. The vice-president and top negotiator for our German affiliate, the 500,000-strong IG Chemie-Papier-Keramik, journeyed to Turkey to counsel with the union. In addition to sending strike funds, the Hoechst union council wired their pledge of solidarity to their Turkish colleagues. As a result of the pressures by the German union, discussions took place at the

115

company's headquarters in Frankfurt which helped lay the basis for a very successful conclusion after a ninety-day strike.

'In both cases a local dispute between comparatively weak unions with limited members and finance and giant multinational corporations was "internationalized". Instead of dealing in isolation from a position of weakness as had always been the case, the union's position was strengthened internationally. It can be predicted with certainty that similar actions will become standard procedure within the ICF as the programme develops.'

The ICF headquarters are in Geneva, along with the other major international labour groups, the International Metalworkers' Federation (IMF), and the International Union of Food and Allied Workers' Associations (IUF). A large part of their armament consists of information, with bulging dossiers on international companies and their financial performance worldwide. The IUF includes Nestlé as an object of study and has used its data file to help in union action against Nabisco. Its plans include a Geneva meeting of union representatives of subsidiaries of Nestlé, Nabisco, and Wagon-Lits.

A classic example of the strategic use of data brought the French St Gobain glass company into dispute with Levinson's ICF and the national unions of France, Germany, Italy and the United States. A meeting of union representatives in Geneva established a battle plan in which national tactics were to be co-ordinated into international strategy. Although the French communist-led union broke away to arrive at its own settlement, the ranks held elsewhere. Satisfactory agreements were reached in Germany and Italy, contingent on acceptable settlements in all countries involved except France. When the company, quite correctly, told its American union that its business was running at a loss, the ICF furnished information showing that St Gobain was profitable worldwide and the American union maintained its claim successfully. According to Mr Levinson:

'The settlements reached in Germany, Italy and the United States were very successful. For example in the U.S. the company was forced to concede increases of $8\frac{1}{2}$ per cent per year during a three-year contract on the basis of its world profits, despite the absence of profits in the United States during the preceding two years. Plant-level bargaining was won in Italy. Important advances in job security were won in

Germany. Further joint actions of this kind are being made ready with selected companies in the chemical, rubber and paper industries.'

The St Gobain incident occurred in 1969. Mr Levinson's prediction bore fruit in February 1972 when, in concert with the IUF, his ICF called a meeting in Geneva of union delegates from nine European countries to draw up a programme on behalf of the 60,000 worldwide employees of the chemical-based conglomerate, W. R. Grace of the U.S. In the words of the meeting's resolution, the Grace company was alleged to have contravened the rules of fair and open bargaining by

'. . . buying and selling companies at a frantic rate, exploiting the advantages of setting up base companies in tax havens for the purpose of hiding profits and thereby understating the contributions of the workers to the earnings of the corporation.'

One of the aims of the union campaign, therefore, is to be informed in advance of the company's investment and divestment plans because these can endanger the job security of workers in the companies involved. To carry out the plan the unions established a 'permanent world-council' which is to set the pattern for other councils to co-ordinate union negotiations with other multinational chemical giants such as Switzerland's Ciba-Geigy and Hoffman-La Roche.

The goal of Levinson and like-minded union leaders is still far from attainment, although the progress made over the past three years in-dicates that it may not always be beyond reach. There are difficult obstacles to overcome. Nationalism is one which makes it difficult to foresee when British unions, for example, will make sacrifices to aid German workers or when either will walk off their jobs to support the better-paid Americans. The pattern, if any, is further disrupted by the communist unions in France and Italy with central offices in Prague. And unless the terminal dates of contracts internationally can be harmonized, common action will encounter the restrictions of legal obstacles in many countries to sympathy strikes.

All these obstructions and more are synthesized in the field of auto-mobile manufacturing, an industry which girdles the globe and which contains both companies and unions with an international viewpoint. The difficulty of common union action is highlighted in a summary printed in *Business Week* headed 'The Problems in Global Bargaining'.

117

'In the *U.S.* the UAW (United Auto Workers) has almost 100 per cent of all U.S. auto workers in its fold. Elsewhere:

'In *Japan* the auto workers are highly unionized but are in seven unions for seven companies. Consolidation efforts began in 1972. Traditionally workers have been unionized on a factory by factory basis. The auto industry would like to keep it that way.

'In *Britain* the unions are craft oriented and politically oriented. There are sixteen in the auto industry, representing perhaps 85 per cent of all auto workers. They bargain jointly with some employers, separately with others, and relations are archaic by U.S. standards.

'In *France* there are no auto unions as such. Auto workers are in four general unions, politically rather than industrially organized. Leaders say France would be "a very poor hunting ground" for organizing global bargaining or auto-union collaboration.

'In *Sweden* all workers in a plant are in a single union, one of three for industrial workers. But the form of Swedish contract bargaining – between unions and federations of employers – would stand in the way of international collaboration of unions.

'In *Italy* some 30 per cent of all auto workers are in four unions – all politically oriented. Three are divisions of a national metalworking union; the fourth, in Fiat, is an independent.

'In *West Germany* auto unionism is closer to the UAW form but is highly nationalistic and company-oriented.'[1]

Despite such obstacles, the move toward international collaboration of organized labour has shown tangible signs of growth. It is being strengthened by the advances in communications which quickly advise labour in one country of gains won by its counterpart in another. Multinational firms must match the awareness of their workers and do this through their managers in the field who report on developments in their areas, and who should be apprised by the parent company of new situations in other countries which may inspire efforts toward change in their own. The role of the manager abroad in the company's communications system thereby takes on added importance, but even the internationalism of labour will not leave him with merely the responsibilities of a reporting officer.

[1] *Business Week*, July 24, 1971.

He will continue to carry a dual role in his relationship with his own workforce: that of representative of the parent company and that of local chief officer. The two postures intermingle inevitably. The local man in the field who uses the home office as an excuse for carrying out unpopular local measures will soon be found out by his subordinates. They will then suspect him for the deceit and downgrade him for his weakness. Some managers carry the stratagem to the point where staff and worker loyalty are affected and they often do this unconsciously. If the manager's attitude toward the parent company is truly hostile, if his suspicions of the executives at headquarters are obvious, the staff which is loyal to him comes to share his hostility and suspicions. Then the loyalty of the local workforce toward the local manager becomes a weak point in the total company fabric. There is little doubt that the field manager strengthens his own position by upholding his company and expressing his differences with headquarters policy in the most discreet and confidential manner.

There will be many occasions for such differences in policy toward personnel. They will start with the manager's immediate subordinates who often have management potential and who are the most vocal representatives of the company in the local community. If they are local nationals, as they usually are, but the parent company concerns itself with them, as it usually does, the local manager may have to intercede effectively on their behalf: to ensure that they are not treated as second-class citizens and to guarantee that they are not encouraged in unrealizable expectations. A company can create no more virulent enemy in its midst than the local submanager whose aspirations are consistently foiled by a stream of home office appointments to the top jobs. Potentially he can resemble the faithful family retainer who one day helps the revolutionaries cut the family's throats.

The next crucial level of personnel relations for the local manager is supervisory. A strongly knit work group, in office or plant, will always try to win over its supervisors and a strong company will always try to hold them on management's side. The manager in the field must have the leadership to defend the company's interests without diminishing the effectiveness of his support staff as supervisors. If these supervisors are nationals of the headquarters country, the issue is settled but the complexities of working with the local staff are multiplied and must be approached with considerable personal guidance on the part of the

119

manager and help from some local staff who may properly expect in their turn to join the management team.

The point is clearly emphasized by Ted R. Brannen and Frank X. Hodgson in their book *Overseas Management*:[2]

'Every individual employs relations with other people as a means of satisfying his needs. Local employees co-operate spontaneously with their overseas supervisors when doing so appears to offer a means of satisfying their needs. Overseas supervisors who understand the needs their local subordinates are attempting to satisfy from their employment and who take an interest in helping to satisfy those needs usually obtain co-operation and acceptable employee performance. On the other hand overseas managers who evidence little interest in helping local employees satisfy their needs usually discover that their local subordinates are not particularly interested in contributing to an efficient operation.'

In summary, *Overseas Management* says,

'In order to qualify as competent overseas managers, as differentiated from competent domestic managers, specialists from industrial nations must be able to satisfy five related responsibilities. They must understand the important characteristics of the local cultural pattern. They must adjust their own attitudes and behaviour to the local cultural environment. They must understand the self-images of employees whose cultural backgrounds are different from their own. They must be able to contribute to the process of modifying the self-images of local employees. And they must be able to contribute effectively to the process of satisfying the needs and expectations of the local subordinates.'

These requirements, of course, pertain primarily to the field of labour relations. One may be permitted to add a sixth: that the manager attain an awareness of the world he lives in, keeping clearly in mind that it includes the multinational world, the world of his local community, and the world of the subsidiary he is managing. There are other worlds with which he must also contend and we will deal with them shortly.

[2] Ted R. Brannen, Frank X. Hodgson, *Overseas Management*, McGraw-Hill, 1965.

Chapter 8

Communications

An old South African song describes a parent's advice to his daughter when receiving a suitor at home as to 'keep on talking'. Then he, when elsewhere in the house, would not worry over whether the young couple were engaging in other activities. This often seems to represent the attitude of home offices towards their managers in the field and it takes the form of requiring a steady stream of reports on all phases of their operations abroad. To many companies this flow of reports represents a communications system.

To the manager abroad it may represent something else. It may be a burden on his time and office resources. It may be a denial of the company's declared policy of decentralization. It is a system of controls. When the information forwarded fulfils the home office requirements but does not include what he would like to say, it is a reporting system but not a communications system. And when the home office receives, but does not acknowledge or comment on, the information the process becomes somewhat like shouting down a well.

To be sure, communications are essential to the co-ordination of a multinational system and vital to certain controls which it must contain. But to stop there or even to elaborate on that concept alone is an uninspired view and one which can nullify the competitive advantages of the international company. Such a company goes abroad because it can compete in foreign markets with superior products or services, or new products and services. When the home office ceases to communicate with the field about these advantages, and about new ones that are being developed, the nerve ends of the system can dry up. Local competitors and other companies maintaining a better dialogue soon make the company old-fashioned. This happens only rarely because in spite of the failings of most international corporate communications systems, the new products and new processes keep coming. The companies therefore survive, but often their managers abroad fall by the wayside. As David Heenan has said:

'Headquarters controls, as communicative devices, enable the international organization to bridge the gap between the head office and its overseas subsidiaries. In addition they insure an appropriate amount of uniformity and consistency among local affiliates. However, over-extensive controls in global corporations will tend to deny operational authority to subsidiary management teams. Instead of overcoming the obstacles to international communications, elaborate control systems impede the development of expatriate managers . . .

'Besides the limitations on autonomy and job content, there is a tendency for headquarters to overlook the need for communication with its overseas personnel. The expatriate's exclusion from the mainstream of corporate life makes informational support all the more necessary to lessen the many uncertainties that cloud the overseas career.'[1]

Corporate communication channels can easily become clogged, and do. There is a tendency to combat the piling up of reports, memos and telexes by responding to each as infrequently as possible. But inevitably, on both ends of the headquarters field-line, the question comes up, 'Why don't they tell us what we want to know?' Since most companies do not even take the trouble to assign communications officers to the problem, there is little prospect that the solution will come out of the parent office and once again the field manager must be astute enough to set the pace. This is not to say that home office aid is impossible.

One recalls the brilliant device of the U.S. Navy in setting up communications with its intelligence posts abroad during the Second World War, most of these posts being manned by men newly drawn from civilian life. They were informed as to what kind of reports were expected and were told not to report when there was nothing to say. At regular periods Washington responded with a bulletin containing thumbnail accounts of the various reports received, with brief comments. Each field office could then not only read commentaries on its own reporting but could compare these comments with headquarters

---

[1] David A. Heenan, 'The Corporate Expatriate: Assignment to Ambiguity', *Columbia Journal of World Business*, May–June 1970.

opinions about reports from colleagues in other posts. These statements alone provided a continual feedback on how each field post was performing. By seeing what the others were doing each post received new ideas and stimulation. Also, an inevitable sense of competition was instilled, as each office wanted to be represented in Washington's bulletin with the best comments possible. There were no critical declarations, incidentally. Some reports were merely noted. Others were described as 'excellent', 'interesting', 'informative', and so on. The Washington bulletin provided a sense of belonging to a lively organization. It was not exhortatory but it was suggestive. Above all it was stimulating to men who, torn from their usual patterns of life, could well have felt forgotten and lonely and who could have wondered why they were writing reports at all. The bulletins had the opposite effect. They formed a sense of teamwork, competitive but friendly and, without seeming to be, they were a training tool. Some company internal house organs attempt to accomplish the same purpose but fail because they are cluttered with other company news and are not a direct response.

Basically there are two types of communication between a home office and the field: operational and informative. There should be no reason for discussion about the first. If operational communications are not effective, neither will operations be. A field man who cannot elicit a prompt response on product specifications, parts supply, or funding capabilities, is working for the wrong company. A company which cannot quickly find out what its field manager is doing to overcome a budget deficit or meet local legal restrictions on packaging, needs another manager. Unfortunately these situations do arise and companies creak through them, while managers endure. One continues to believe that the establishment of communications officers to police this kind of traffic would save time, money, and men. The idea is not obscure merely because most companies have been blind to it. In simple terms this requires the appointment of someone at the home office to receive requests from the field for information, with that same person to pass back to the field the home office's demands for data or statements about affairs abroad. In either instance, this traffic officer acts to ensure that responses are prompt. However, the traffic man must not be a bottleneck; communications should be allowed to bypass this facility when either end of the line has established another direct channel of communication. In other words, the traffic manager of home office-field communications is there to facilitate contact, not to block it for his own purposes.

This position can be creative. It can take on the task of ensuring that the field receives certain information which might be overlooked by others in the company. It can, for example, pass on copies of published notices about the company. It can, when authorized, forward information about major personnel changes or developments concerning client relationships. It can, having acquired an understanding of the field's needs, ensure that the subsidiary company's manager knows about relevant developments in the company before his clients or competitors do. Nothing is more maddening to a field manager than to have clients, competitors, and others in his industry tell him what is happening in his own company. He is truly in this respect the husband who knows last and whereas, like the husband, he may forgive the act, he can never pardon having been the last to know – properly so, for this undermines his position. The alert communications officer at headquarters, if there is one, would avert such a situation. More positively, this officer would put our man in the field in the position of being in advance of the news, and ahead of competitors, clients and suppliers.

The Interpublic Group of Companies, a worldwide network of advertising agencies serving such clients as Esso, Coca-Cola and General Motors, has made good use of just such a service to its field and domestic offices. By requiring that requests for information and technical assistance be channelled through a single person at headquarters, it has eliminated a great deal of waste in intracompany communications. The system prevents field officers from bothering domestic specialists directly. It works to formulate requests clearly and to avoid replies asking for more detail. It also averts the kind of duplication which might be caused when an office in Milan and one in Manila happen to need the same kind of data or help. The process also trains the communications officer – who actually acts as a switchboard operator taking calls and plugging them in to the proper source for replies – to learn the idiosyncrasies of the field officers and their requirements. With this accumulated background, the communications officer then becomes qualified to initiate a flow of appropriate information to the field and to institute a programme of regular mailings that help the field offices match the performance of the domestic personnel by virtue of sharing their knowledge.

124

The Interpublic system also spotlights the field manager as the key factor in intracompany communications, when it becomes apparent that some field offices make intelligent use of the service and others either ignore it or fail to grasp its potential worth to them. Some offices seize on the material mailed from the parent company as the subject for staff training meetings or as news of interest to local clients, prospects, and the trade press. Others merely file it. It becomes evident that a piece concerning a new marketing technique is only as useful as its reader makes it. Some fail to realize its potential; others give it added value by using it well and ingeniously.

The system works to facilitate the exchange of information but not to obstruct the necessary open lines of contact between field management and its domestic counterparts when the subject is a management decision, or one concerning service to an international client, or the pursuit of an international prospect. Here again both ends of the line have the responsibility to let the other know what is required.

Most companies realize that personal contact between their domestic and field men is needed to facilitate coherent operations. Whereas this calls for travel abroad, and occasional visits to the home office from the field, time and cost preclude reaching an optimum level of such contact and so company management meetings are brought into play.

These gatherings of managers, usually under the aegis of the parent company, have their value points and their disadvantages. They provide an excellent arena for the distribution of information, exchange of ideas, updating of field (and domestic) management, evaluation of the men involved, and the opportunity for personal contact which can sharpen later communication between the field and the home office and between the field offices themselves. A carefully-planned meeting that stays with its agenda – hopefully one to which all participants have contributed in advance – and which includes definite goals to be achieved is invaluable. One of the most important side effects of such meetings is the informal exchange between field managers during the assembly's leisure moments. These often result in unwritten agreements to keep in touch on the subject of company resources, which can advance the growth of the offices concerned.

If some evils endemic to so many of these meetings are allowed to break in, they are best abandoned. The meeting held for the purpose of exalting a home office chief and his staff usually achieves the opposite effect. If such a meeting exudes luxury in its trappings when field managers have been under heavy pressure to cut expenses and develop profits, it is more of an irritant than a stimulant. Too often, also, field managers are asked to contribute to these meetings in order to be subjected to parent company evaluation. Sensing this, the managers are apt to attempt to impress rather than inform, and the competitive spirit engendered can become savage. Then of course there are the sales meetings which build a carnival atmosphere neither worthy of the company nor the men in it. Usually they include some fatalities in the form of overexuberant spirits who are later dropped from the company.

The most acceptable formula, and one which many companies are making their own, is a two-tier set of meetings: one bringing regional managers together with the parent officers, the other joining the various regions in their own assemblies. In both cases the meetings are usually more businesslike, but to give full value to the regional gatherings those assembled should have some assurance that they have a pipeline to the home office, either through the stature of the regional manager or through the presence of a parent company representative.

No discussion of international communications can avoid the prickly question of language. Within their own companies most international firms have made English the common language. This includes the Scandinavian and the Dutch companies, but exceptions are the Japanese and most of the French companies. With the growing trend towards appointment of local nationals to field management, the problem tends to grow rather than diminish. Businesses concerned with engineering and technical products have an easier time, as their glossaries are more specific and education in these fields has a strong English bias. But the service industries – advertising, consultancy, banks, hotels, and others – must usually require English as a management qualification. This is only a partial solution because the use of language is more subjective in such concerns, calling for careful written work and even more care in conversation.

Ideally the field manager acquires a knowledge of the language of his area, but he does so at his own risk. In France, and in the Paris region particularly, there is little sympathy for anyone speaking less than perfect French. In most other countries even a faltering effort will bring the local listener over to one's side, but awareness of one's shortcomings and the plentiful use of disclaimers is advisable. An experience of mine in Argentina illustrates the point. An Argentine client usually preferred to speak English with me, if only to demonstrate that he knew the language. But if the matter under discussion was one where he sought to gain an advantage he reverted to Spanish, requiring me to do the same. Although the tactics gave my adversary a slight edge, it also flashed me a signal to tread carefully, somewhat nullifying his advantage.

Many company meetings use simultaneous translation facilities, but they are appropriate only for presentations to large audiences. Discussion dies and exchange is never born. Inability to conduct a company meeting in a single language, well understood by all, cuts out one of the major derivative benefits of such a meeting – the capacity of those attending to play back the content of the meeting to their own office when they return. This can be overcome by later delivering to each office a transcribed record of the proceedings, but this is expensive and the discussion will lose many valuable nuances.

The manager who can easily absorb the content of a company meeting, then translates it back to his staff in their own national language, becomes a stalwart pinion of his company's communication system, while strengthening his leadership over his own post. The other, the manager who knows little of the local language and makes little effort to overcome the handicap, puts himself under artificial restraints. He must reach his workforce through local bilingual spokesmen and hope that they are translating his thoughts accurately and without subjective colouration. A certain shyness is self-imposed; it often is misinterpreted as aloofness, or vacillation, or downright weakness. In a sense such a manager abdicates one of the tools and prerogatives of management: effective communication. Of course, he can take the point of view that his staff bear the responsibility of understanding him, or he will find a staff that can. However, in taking this attitude the manager is merely sheltering under a managerial weakness of arrogance. It also directs his staff's energies from the prime attribute a manager wants in his subordinates: effectiveness.

The manager as communicator can act as a multiplier of effectiveness, or as an inhibitor. When, by setting an example, he persuades a staff of the value of in-company communications, he can stimulate lower levels to exchange ideas and help freely. If he is inept, or unwilling to engage in free discussions of the work at hand, the staff below him may well decide on an 'every man for himself' policy. Recognition of this concept has caused many companies to change their physical establishments into open areas, abandoning the classic closed-door offices.

Summing up the role of the manager abroad as an intracompany communicator, he is the bridge between his workforce and the home office, transmitting to each the strengths of the other. He is also an educator, teaching the parent company the intricacies of his environment, its opportunities and its demands, while bringing back to his own area the product benefits, technology, and methodology which his parent company can contribute. By responding promptly and decisively to his home office he hopes to elicit similar responses to his own queries and suggestions. With an alert ear for any local business news which can add to the parent company's knowledge of its global environment, he makes himself a valued intelligence officer. In doing so, he must resist the temptation to broadcast memos throughout domestic ranks to further his own political designs in the company. Patiently but insistently he must attempt to create within the home office an awareness of the benefits of a well-organized flow of information. The process may be slow because parent companies tend towards management by exception, dealing only with what seems obviously to concern them. But there are techniques for achieving the result and one of them is to acknowledge promptly the receipt of useful information and follow through with a report to the home office on how it has been utilized.

The other facet of the manager's communications responsibilities deals with the world outside the company. In part his own judgement must be his guide, but in his representation of the company the manager should seek agreement on the image the firm desires. A common definition should mean one to which the manager contributes in his assessment of the local scene and of his evaluation of the way in which the company image should be presented locally.

In the highly-developed industrial atmosphere of Europe, a multinational company may best enter the scene by openly proclaiming its international stance which supports its product benefits and advanced technology. But where product performance will depend heavily on expert local service, the integration of the company into the local economy should be emphasized. In the sensitive less-developed countries which display a high level of nationalism, some international companies attempt to camouflage themselves with local colouration, although rarely with notable success. If any of their customers are international firms, the chameleon role is usually counter-productive, as it plays down the firm's multinational resources. Some international advertising agencies sell their internationalism to multinational clients while proclaiming their local orientation (local personnel, length of time in the area, etc.) to local businesses. This sleight of hand rarely works. Usually, on the contrary, it would be best to tell the international prospect how 'local' they have become while impressing local firms with their international resources.

Every international firm states that it intends to be a good corporate citizen in the host country, developed or not. Usually the declaration is fatuous because even most of the local firms fall short of that objective. They are the first to cast a jaundiced eye on the efforts of the intruder to be holier than they are, which it often is in terms of more liberal personnel policies, better service, guarantee of product quality, and sometimes generosity in support of community projects. The local manager walks a narrow path here but if he treads it with care local business, he may be sure, will ultimately imitate his company's success.

Perhaps his best choice, when he has one, is to be virtuous but not to talk too much about it. He should advise against self-congratulatory advertising. Many a multinational firm tells us what it is doing to 'make this a better world for you' while spewing pollutants over the earth. If a local manager does find opportunities to make contributions to the local community's welfare, let him remember that the key technique of good public relations is the third-party endorsement. If he has persuaded the home office to grant his request for air-conditioning in the local plant, let him see to it that the labour organizers spread the word about it. If he has been able to make a contribution to the local business school, let the educators carry the story to the public, especially if they want further assistance. If he stands firm against a monopoly distribution system, and breaks through, let the independent retailers blow the horn. One of the few individual American industrialists to establish a consistently successful record of dealings with South American governments mystified his competitors as to his technique, which naturally brought about accusations of nefarious practices. Perhaps he was no less blameless than the others, but his

129

secret was an ability to find the local nationals who would know how to speak for him.

This brings to mind the press, which is ever with us. Many managers abroad operate without good press relations men on their staff, and some with none. For one reason, good press relations men are hard to find anywhere, and abroad they often work under the illusion that their effectiveness depends on their important contacts or on the amount of glorification they can achieve for their employers, and some managers encourage this fantasy.

Regrettably, the press has done little or nothing to advise business of how it wants to be treated. One would think that a book, or articles, or press-business seminars on the press viewpoint in its relations with business would make life easier for both sides. Nevertheless, there are a few rules which an astute manager in the field may follow in his relationships with the local press.

First he should inform himself as to the nature of the local press. Is it independent or does it serve one faction or another and, if the latter, what are the goals of the factions? Is it free, and if not what is the extent of government controls on it? Is it nationalistic? Is it prosperous or can it be bought – particularly by adversaries? What is its attitude towards business, particularly towards local business and multinational enterprises? How likely is a publication to put a sensational bias on the news? Finally, a manager should obtain an assessment of the influence of the press in the community.

This type of inquiry is important but it may have the unfortunate effect of making the manager excessively wary of the local press. Wary he may be, but that should not be apparent. A newsman's livelihood is news and respect for that fact will avoid misunderstanding. Deceit will never be forgiven for it endangers the newsman's job and his publication's credibility. Rather than put a reporter off or mislead him it is advisable, if need be, to tell him the subject is not up for discussion now but he will be advised when it is. Even this tactic must be scrutinized, for the refusal to answer a question can be reported negatively, so the refusal must be carefully framed. 'We are preparing a statement on that and you will have it as soon as it is ready', may be an appropriate answer to a reporter's question. This will not ensure that the reporter will drop the story. He may very well try to pry it out of another member of the company. Therefore there should be a clear understanding within the company that only certain designated officers are authorized to speak to the press.

One danger to avoid whenever possible is the telephone interview. Once a reporter puts a question on the phone he controls the interview, perhaps obtaining the information he wants without including what the manager wants him to know. In such instances he should be invited to the company's offices for a talk.

The technique of making announcements to the press calls for recognition of its competitive nature. If the news is important it should be made simultaneously available to all local journals and provided either in a mailed or personally distributed written release or in a press conference open to all. Press conferences should be the exception. They take up a newsman's time and they are such an overworked method that they are regarded with some scepticism. The best occasions for press conferences are those where (1) the subject is probably better clarified in a question-and-answer session; (2) there is something to show or demonstrate, a product, a process, a new wing on the factory, a laboratory innovation; or where (3) an important visiting company official has something interesting to say. Press conferences are useful but have their drawbacks. If the news involved is dull or merely serving to promote the company, the next conference may be poorly attended. If there is a bigger and unforeseen news break elsewhere – resignation or appointment of a government official, a big business failure, or any accident or incident of urgent news interest – the carefully planned conference fails. The reporters have been called elsewhere. If company representatives at the conference are not carefully prepared for all questions or if they are careless in informal chats over coffee or scotch afterwards, the conference may yield surprising news.

In general the company's relationship with the press should be guided by a willingness to be helpful to the journals and their reporters, and not merely by a desire to use them for the company's own ends. Respect for other people's businesses usually leads to the best way to gain respect and good representation for one's own.

131

Chapter 9

Citizen of What?

The manager abroad who casually announces himself a citizen of the world might well prepare to answer further questions. What world or worlds? During his career the questions will recur, if only in his own mind. His allegiances will be continually challenged by virtue of his association with a multinational organization assailed by the conflicting demands of nations and factions throughout the world.

One such company, solid, successful and seemingly indestructible, is General Motors. Its subsidiary in South Africa has been in operation for forty-four years, yet as recently as March 1972 the company was relieved to hear that Roy Wilkins, moderate and prestigious leader of the black civil-rights movement in the United States had declared that General Motors should not withdraw from South Africa. Wilkins contended that GM's presence in South Africa is better for the coloured population there than its absence would be. It is employing coloured workers, paying them well in relation to local wage scales and training them for better jobs. Its withdrawal would symbolize protest against South Africa's apartheid policy but would not do anything tangible for the coloureds. Yet that withdrawal had been demanded by the U.S. Episcopal Church at a GM stockholders' meeting. In this case, although the local GM manager's advice was undoubtedly influential and his position in South African circles delicate, the final decision rests with the home office.

The contrary seems to be the case in the instance of a British international company in Rhodesia. The company is Aspro-Nicholas and its subsidiary in Salisbury is Nicholabs (Proprietary) Ltd. According to the English newspaper, the *Sunday Times*, during the investigation of the Pearce Commission concerning the proposed independence agreement in Rhodesia, the Salisbury management of Nicholabs sent the following letter to its African workers:

'Dear Sir,

As a Rhodesian who is well employed by a company which is world-wide, I wish to advise that I am in agreement with the proposals for settlement as I feel it would be in the best interests for the future of Rhodesia if a settlement could be reached and do *not* wish to be associated with the violence and unrest at present amongst certain troublemakers in the country.'

Upon being questioned on the matter, a company official in London said the letter was 'obviously local management initiative.' In any case the Salisbury management will be forced to carry that responsibility henceforth, regardless of what may occur in Rhodesia.

To date American multinational companies have felt domestic pressures more than others – from the government in its efforts to control the outflow of dollars and in its historical restrictions on the shipment of strategic goods to the Eastern bloc, as well as in the reach of anti-trust regulations; but it has also felt pressures from minority racial and church groups, some of whom are stockholders. Companies of other nations are not exempt from similar pressures, although they may presently be mild. The British in Africa are an instance. The Swedish companies are vulnerable because of that nation's traditional inclination towards moral judgements on the actions of other nations, i.e. the U.S. in Vietnam. And with all companies being held responsible for the growth of worldwide pollution, this may be only the opening wedge of public domestic concern with the activities of international companies abroad.

An instance of such pressure nearly foreclosing a company's activities in a foreign state again involves South Africa and an American company, Polaroid. The problem and its solution have been reported by Business International as follows:

'. . . U.S. based companies are probably the most likely targets for such pressures. A recent case in point is that of Polaroid of the U.S. which has no direct investment in South Africa but sells cameras and films through an independent distributor and has a licensee manufacturing Polaroid sunglasses. Polaroid has made conscientious efforts to recruit and train black Americans and has made significant contributions for the improvements of black communities in the U.S.

'But, starting last fall, a half-dozen of Polaroid's black employees at

133

headquarters organized a series of demonstrations demanding that the company stop selling in South Africa, announce its policy on apartheid, and turn over its South African profits to revolutionary groups. The group accused Polaroid of supporting apartheid because its South African distributor, Frank & Hirsch, supplies film for the South African government's identification card system (the notorious passbooks that sparked the Sharpeville massacre of blacks in 1960).

'Polaroid could have easily withdrawn from the South African market because its sales there represent less than one-half of one per cent of worldwide sales. Instead it chose to stay but also to study the problem of apartheid by sending a biracial committee (two whites and two blacks) to South Africa, and it ordered a halt to all sales to the South African government.

'Polaroid's committee was granted South African visas and allowed to travel freely in the country, where it met with an across-the-board representation of blacks and whites. The overwhelming attitude on the part of South African blacks and liberal whites was that Polaroid's withdrawal could not help, but that only by staying could the company help ease the social division of the country. After the committee's return, Polaroid issued a plan of action to aid black education and upgrade black wages and is urging other foreign companies to join in. The main points of its programme include:

'– The distributor will substantially raise salaries and other benefits for blacks.

'– As a condition of continuing as Polaroid's licensee, South African Sunglasses will be required to institute a training programme for black employees.

'– Polaroid will commit a portion of its South African profits to black education and a grant of R10,100 is being given to the black-run Association for Education and Cultural Advancement.

'– It will also give a grant to a South African foundation (perhaps the Institute of Race Relations) to underwrite educational expenses of about five hundred local black students. Polaroid will also support two exchange fellowships for blacks under the U.S.-South African Leader Exchange Programme.

'Although the South African government has protested that Polaroid is interfering with its domestic policies, it has made no move to impede the biracial mission and has stated that it will not block Polaroid's

134

programme. It is apparent that the South African government wants to avoid a confrontation with foreign business over its racial policies.'

On occasion the pressure flows in the other direction, as when companies become vulnerable to expropriation and seek the protection of their home governments, or when the world's oil producers confront escalating demands from countries granting concessions for drilling, or when the home country's foreign policy endangers the economic future of companies in a particular country, which occurred when the United States supported Pakistan in its struggle with India over Bangladesh. American businessmen in India protested about the policy to Washington, not only because they thought it wrong but because the subsequent irritation of Indian authorities would make it harder for Americans to do business in India. In South America, American business has long claimed that it has no political aims and only seeks a 'friendly climate of free enterprise'. Washington embraced the concept, fruitlessly of course, because the climate for free enterprise is usually a political and ideological product.

So what world endows the manager abroad with its citizenship? He does not abandon his own country, to which he is further tied by loyalty to the home company. (The exception is the local national manager, whose loyalty to his own country may be challenged on occasion by the requirements of a multinational employer.) Strange changes of attitude occur in the case of the expatriate, often without his being aware. Traditionally the political leanings of the expatriate business community have been conservative, Republican if they are Americans, Tory if British, etc. Although some of the new generation of overseas managers bring more liberal views into the overseas community, they also often tend towards the conservative view which makes it difficult for them to understand the radicalism they often encounter overseas, whether it takes the shape of Indian or Swedish socialism or the instability of African and Latin American states.

The process of gaining understanding and tolerance has its odd concomitants. After some years at it, the overseas manager often finds that he is concerned about public affairs only as they affect his business; otherwise he has become uncommitted. Since he has no electoral vote and properly cannot become politically involved in his new country he moves, in a sense, free of both involvement with the political affairs

135

of his own country, from which he has become estranged, and of the new one. In other words, he veers toward a void. This is when he begins to talk about being a citizen of the world because in his heart he wonders whether he is a citizen of any state at all. This doubt often makes him critical of his own country. Wanting it to do the right thing always, because he still wears its label, he becomes quite intolerant of its political blunders and positively enraged at its errors in the field of foreign policy – for he now has a closer view of the effects of this policy, or thinks he has.

But much depends on his company, its views, and on how close or distant he is to it in terms of visits home, recycling tours of duty at home, and its own degree of liberalism or conservatism. One can well imagine a businessman in Salisbury coming home one evening and telling his wife, 'John brought a queer one to the club today, a fellow from Polaroid. Can you imagine the incredible thing they are doing in South Africa? . . .' For certainly, while ties with home may become shaken but not shattered, the new universe is the host country and the local employees the manager abroad is directing.

The employees are often people with a strange language, and always with strange customs, attitudes, and aspirations. But they become the overseas manager's people and this becomes his world, or one of his worlds. This universe has its component parts, and he must determine how to harmonize with each in order to do his job and live a life of reasonable self-fulfilment. He must learn to move in the company of business associates and competitors, and within that company to advance the ideas of his firm and those of himself while learning what succeeds or fails in the local business milieu. This atmosphere may be one where bribery is a way of life or, as in Switzerland, where honesty is held in high regard but the entire country is 'managed' in ways mysterious to the foreigner who may spend a great deal of time fruitlessly seeking the springs of power.

A third world to which the overseas manager belongs is the local colony of his countrymen, who have their American Club, English Club, Swedish, Dutch, or Swiss Society, or whatever it may be. The extent of his association with this group calls for careful measurement, for to plunge into its comfortable atmosphere of like-minded, like-tongued compatriots may mean he is isolating himself from the people of the host country, and it is usually with the latter that he must do

136

business. The expatriate club has a parallel, generally in the expatriate residential section. In Geneva the United Nations people usually live on one side of Lake Leman and the expatriate businessmen on the other. The Genevese are scattered throughout but their business leaders have their own enclaves. In Buenos Aires the foreign community lives in the northern suburbs, observing each other's every move in an atmosphere of cheery informality that often pierces the barriers of privacy. In Rio de Janeiro, Copacabana and Ipanema beaches are still the haunts of foreign residents. In Manila, it is Forbes Park. In each case, residence in one of these areas, pleasant as it may be, marks the foreigner as having made a decision to live amongst his own nationals rather than with the natives. On the other hand, a decision not to join one of these compounds may be criticized by one's compatriots. Often, an acceptable compromise may be found in choosing to live in the neighbourhood of foreigners from another country – an Englishman with Swedes, a Hollander with Americans – which often internationalizes a man and frees him from the grasp of his countrymen. The international qualities of the executive can be further accented by joining one or two good local clubs as well as his national one, and yet further emphasized if his wife finds friends from various countries while his children are educated at a local school. Such a pattern, not always wholly possible, usually enriches the experience of living abroad and adds style to the manager's operations.

This process of integration into the host community has its interesting twists and turns and some quite pleasant surprises. The overseas manager and his family often find themselves selecting from their new life those facets which delight them while they learn to build defences against the others. They may find French food an enchanting experience while observing the country's politics with disdain. Or they may be pleased with the manners of the French socially and commercially while shuddering at the savagery of the same people at the wheel of a car. London's theatre life makes addicts of visiting Americans who are driven to the point of near madness by the deliberate pace of the city's businessmen. Mexico's charms unfold endlessly while at the same time its functionaries can become irritating with their demands for a 'bite' of cash before acting.

More important in our discussion is what effect the overseas experience has on an executive directing a foreign subsidiary. This will

137

depend considerably on where he is assigned and what he does to overcome unfavourable circumstances or to take advantage of opportunities. If he is moved from a highly industrialized to a less-developed country, he runs the risk of deterioration. This is aggravated when his company tends toward a high degree of centralization. In this situation the manager may become merely a company representative in a comfortable but unstimulating atmosphere. Without competitive challenges and with his thinking done for him at home office, this manager can succumb to sloth while allowing the subsidiary's profit and loss statement to reassure him that he is on the mark. This idyllic existence has its charms but behind them rests the threat that the manager is falling behind and will never regain the thrust needed to advance his career.

There are various responses to such a situation. On the cultural level there is the country's language to learn, its history to explore, and its culture to comprehend. On the assumption that no contemporary society is static there are changes to observe for perspicacious reports to the parent company, such the as shifts in political inclination, the development of labour relations, the social shifts that will alter market patterns, the pressures on currency, the growth or regression of the country's capacity to join the club of developed nations.

On a business level the manager can look for opportunities for new products and additional services. Probably his workforce will be functioning under the handicaps of inexperience and less-advanced production facilities, and his skills can be applied to overcoming these drawbacks. He may sharpen his technical skills to boost production and his human sensitivities to promote training of his staff and workers. Devising effective training programmes can and should be a major portion of the manager's job abroad, particularly where labour is largely unskilled and the staff have only an elementary knowledge of business procedures. The teaching process can tighten the tie between the manager abroad and his home office, for he will have the right to request all possible help from the parent company in providing teaching materials and in packaging the training programmes which he will have to comprehend and administer. Bringing these programmes into being will strengthen his local relationships with organized labour and usually with the local government authorities as well.

By training local employees and bringing those at higher levels up for submanagement and eventual management responsibilities, the director of the foreign affiliate usually opens new areas of contact and activity. The problems of personnel training are often shared by other businesses, national as well as multinational, and they often join in setting up institutes of business training for local junior executives. Local educators or the local university may also be interested in collaborating with the effort or perhaps taking it over. In this case the manager will often find himself involved as a guest lecturer. The grouping of businesses to train local junior executives has made a significant contribution to the development of an administrative cadre in many less-developed countries, to the benefit of the businesses involved, since this eventually provides a pool of talent on which they can draw. Multinational companies have in the past complained about the costs of their in-company training efforts when other companies took away their newly equipped trainees at higher salaries. The mutual raiding and competition for an insufficient number of junior executives has on occasion created unreasonably high salaries while causing an unhealthy atmosphere of executive mobility. The joining of businesses to bring a class of junior executives into being through out-company programmes has tended to alleviate that problem.

Should the assignment be in Western Europe, the United States or Japan, there is little danger of the manager going to seed. His environment will be intensely competitive, innovative, and fast-paced. Business challenges will be as sharp, or sharper, than in the home office. There may be a similarity in business methods because the techniques of management are transferable from country to country, but management styles differ, as do national cultures. It is in comprehending these styles that the manager abroad in a developed country encounters a dimension of challenge not found at home.

There is finally the question of the manager's own training, which is the responsibility of the parent company. The first stage, of course, is the preparation for the executive's first overseas assignment and there are almost as many views about the proper method as there are multinational companies.

Some companies conduct in-house training programmes in which candidates for overseas assignments are exposed to veterans who have returned from abroad to their home offices. Others send a man out as a junior and let him demonstrate on the job his capabilities for management abroad. One petroleum company sends its men abroad, then

139

brings them back after about six months for a period of intensive training before reassigning them to the field. Others use universities and advanced business schools to break-in their candidates for overseas management. The initial step is the crucial one, for if a man fails on his first overseas assignment he is unlikely to recover the ground or be given another such opportunity.

The cost of such a mis-step is great for the company and disastrous for the man. That companies still send men abroad without first assuring themselves of the executives' ability to cope with the world abroad is rather remarkable. Yet many do, counting on the new managers to repeat overseas the effective domestic performances which may have earned them the assignment. As we have said, this procedure may be costly. It may also be too slow for the pace of contemporary business. The traditional view that a manager's first year abroad should be considered his breaking-in period does not resist the onslaught of insistent competition. The business world will not stand still for a year while a man learns a responsible job and a new way of life.

Recognizing this, a few advanced business schools have established programmes to prepare executives for management abroad. The programmes themselves, to be effective, are long, lasting from two to ten months, but their purpose is to see that their participants are prepared to handle their assignments abroad from the day of arrival. Such programmes, and there are not many of them, include management techniques and study of the contemporary worldwide business environment. They add to the standard management diet of finance, marketing, information systems, general management, and organizational behaviour a seasoning of respect for different national management styles. Small groups and project teams of students of diverse nationalities soon learn that each approaches a problem differently but perhaps equally well. If it is possible for the participant's family to move with him to the city where the school is located, it more faithfully simulates the experience of life abroad. Not all schools, in fact very few, can offer this mix of international teaching in a multinational faculty with an international selection of participants, and a global point of view. They are mostly limited to continental Europe where the CEI in Geneva, INSEAD in Fontainebleau and IMEDE in Lausanne have, in varying degrees, the facilities described.

However, the business community is reaching the view that the first step should be only the beginning of a continuing process. The manager and his company should be on the alert for further opportunities to return to a study atmosphere for shorter courses of one or more weeks for reappraisal and recycling, and there are many more institutions ready and able to provide such courses, primarily in the United States, England, and on the Continent. Many executives up to chairman level make these programmes part of their continuing career development. They also add, when time permits, some of the many seminars that schools, management consultants, and information services offer. In doing so the international executive mixes with the domestic management and with his counterparts. Increasingly, he finds himself exchanging experiences with other international executives.

This becomes for many firms part of a process leading towards the ideal solution of the problem of international management: the creation of a cadre of professional international managers. In the continuing discussion over the relative merits of the home country executive as against the local national as a manager abroad, the third solution is often cited as best, the third-country manager, neither from the home office nor a national of the subsidiary's host country, but a foreigner removed from his own state. In this manager, many of the conflicts of citizenship and divided loyalties are removed. He is simply a professional, working where he may be assigned, not pining for a return home, not fearing another transfer, and with a minimum of emotional attachments to hinder his concentration on the job at hand.

Much of this type of professionalism is gained, however, in the increasing contacts of managers abroad with each other, in schools and seminars, but even more on the job, where they meet at clubs, chambers of commerce, in industrial associations, and informally as they come to know each other and find mutual interests. The sharing of interests, even between competitors, increases a mutuality of understanding, such as that enjoyed by other specialists of different nations – scientists, doctors, lawyers, teachers, dentists, all sharing the international language of their professions. As the multinational world of business grows and takes shape, it will inevitably spawn a class of professional international managers. Some companies – petroleum and mining companies especially – claim to have such men on their payrolls already. For these men the question, 'citizen of what world?', contains an

141

answer: citizen of the world of multinational business. Which leads us, finally, to an analysis of what that world is, for it is a turbulent one and the shape of its future, its problems, its contributions and its responsibilities is changing from an amorphous mass to a recognizable structure, one which will largely determine the role of the multinational man, the manager abroad.

Chapter 10

The Multinational Company

The equivocal character of multinational business has finally been given official recognition by two of the world's major supranational bodies. Both the United Nations and the European Economic Commission have established study committees to tackle the questions of the status of multinational companies in world society, their rights and responsibilities and the regulatory structures that should apply to them.

In all likelihood the United Nations' effort will become bogged down in a morass of international politics with the Western nations, the socialist states and the Third World pouring their own attitudes into the melting pot of international debate, with nothing definable coming out of it.

The EEC is a different matter, however. The homogeneity of the states constituting the Common Market and the restriction of the UN study to their area may make it possible for policies of substance to emerge. It is probable that the different EEC countries will agree to a proposed common policy, at least in part. It is also possible that such a project will provide the impetus for future state-sponsored approaches to the problems of national state relationships with multinational firms.

Although the companies may view this development with some trepidation, they may also accept it with a measure of relief, for the truth is that for too long the multinational corporation has moved in a rarefied and unreal atmosphere.

Although the multinational corporation is applauded as a developer and pioneer of modern business practice, in terms of its relationships with governments it has fallen behind other business policy and practice. The tendencies towards close alliances of domestic business and government have strengthened, while the ties between multinational firms and nation states have become increasingly fragile. The growth

143

of international communities such as the EEC, COMECON, the Central American group, LAFTA in South America, and the Andean group, as well as the incipient effort in black Africa, further complicates the status of the multinational company, although it may clarify the position of the cross-border businesses *within* such groupings. It is not unimaginable that the larger international companies may eventually have to hive off their operations within these national groupings into almost completely autonomous divisions.

Meanwhile, local business everywhere deals ever more closely with its national government. In the socialist states, it is either controlled or owned by the national governments. In Spain, Italy and Portugal, the governments are in business and keeping a watchful eye on their independent competitors. In France, government planning and control of credit sets the pace for business. In Great Britain, one major party sleeps with business while the other, when it can, locks the door so it won't roam the town. In the United States the distance between Washington and Wall Street continually diminishes.

This trend has not been completely unfavourable to business, for as it has permitted government to interfere with business, so it has also allowed business to augment its influence over government.

However, multinational business has grown, and grown astoundingly, outside this thickening web of government-business relationships. In its international operations multinational business increasingly escapes the arm of government control while in its stateless garb its direct influence on government is decreasing.

Half a century ago the status of the multinational company as an international outlaw – to use an extreme term – caused little concern. But its growth and present power now make international business impossible to ignore. On the contrary, it has become a focal point of anxiety for governments, labour, and students of international affairs, and the role assigned to its representatives abroad emerges as an issue calling for definition. About 15 per cent of the gross world product is estimated to constitute the output of international business today. This contribution is reported to be increasing at the rate of 10 per cent per year, well above the rate attained by the average nation state. At the present relative rates of growth, in less than thirty years multinational business will account for one-half or more of the world's gross product.

It is not surprising that under the circumstances some multinational corporations should equate their political power with their economic prowess, an error to which many governments may over-react, as may be the case in the coming United Nations investigation. Indeed, this project was stimulated in large part by the misjudgement of the ITT Corporation when, according to syndicated columnist Jack Anderson,

'... a vice-president of the International Telephone & Telegraph Corporation wrote the White House urging action to make Chile in effect safe for ITT. The Chileans had elected a Socialist, Salvador Allende Gossens, as President, and the New York-based corporation felt that his inauguration should be prevented so as to safeguard ITT and other U.S. investments in Chile and other Latin American countries.'

Whereas Latin American politicians have often in the past denounced foreign corporations for supposed abuses against their sovereignty and their economies, this was one of the most flagrant charges to be made by such allegedly disinterested parties. That it attracted international attention was proved by the appearance of an analysis of the situation which Claude Monnier wrote for Geneva's *Journal de Genève*, March 24, 1972. Mr Monnier stated:

'... if one can without doubt lay the ITT affair to the irresponsibility of some individuals, the basic problem remains: the giant corporations, because they recognize neither borders nor nation states, and can easily move their pawns about the geographic chessboard, doubtless acquire an independence of nation states which amounts almost to disdain.

'As these enterprises are by definition enormous in their own countries and naturally have strong political influence there, there is a good chance that, politically irresponsible, they will engage in parallel political action to force their own government's hand or to support it, as the case may be.

'The government of the home country must, if it wishes to maintain its authority, systematically discourage such amateur diplomacy. And if it wishes to maintain itself in office, it must pitilessly repress such collusion as existed between the CIA and ITT.

'But, finally, the only means of avoiding the potential threat of multinational enterprises is to require that they sink strong roots in each country where they operate and not be at the mercy of every

145

decree from the home office. Otherwise, nothing will keep them under control.'

Mr Monnier does not define the 'strong roots' which he would have international companies sink into the soil of their host countries. ITT had a $200 million investment in Chile, which should have rooted it firmly enough, especially in view of the $39 million annual profit it was said to retrieve from its Chilean operations. But Mr Monnier's second point is clear: that the men in the home office should not project international policy into the affairs of their affiliates abroad. ITT is a highly centralized conglomerate, for all the disparity of its various holdings.

The unfavourable aura that its political manœuvrings cast on the international business scene aroused the interest of the press in further stories based on the sheer power of international companies, and soon there appeared an item in the *International Herald Tribune* highlighting this theme:

'For years the EEC has been considering a tax on soybean imports.

'Although the U.S. government has warned of dire consequences if the tax is imposed (soybeans are a major U.S. farm export) insiders here say the real reason the community has yet to act is the power of Unilever, the U.K.–Dutch-owned fats and oils manufacturer. The tax would increase its manufacturing costs.

' "Wags here call Unilever the seventh member of the EEC. Unilever has no Brussels lobby," says Michael de Courcy, a high official in the commercial section of the EEC Commission. "It doesn't need one – it has the Dutch government." '

The ability of the multinational corporation to take a middle road, joining neither local business on one side nor national governments on the other, makes it a target for such snipers. The Japanese, perhaps more sensitive than others to questions of their image as they move aggressively into the international business community, seem more aware than others that independence is accompanied by vulnerability. Their overriding technique for expansion into other countries is the joint venture method. Whereas companies of other nations tend to withdraw from this option because of its limitations on their independence, the Japanese are willing to trade off some independence for the protective colouration of a joint venture. They may set a trend in this direction.

146

Meanwhile, the manager abroad can take comfort in knowing that the multinational corporation has its adherents, most of them in the ranks of business and the universities, not many in government or the groupings of labour. While this support has not stilled the opposition or quieted those with honest doubts about the contributions of multinational corporations, it is firm and articulate, as statements like the following demonstrate:

'The emergence of the multinational private corporation as a powerful agent of world social and economic change has been a signal development of the postwar era. This evolution has been regarded with mixed opinions by public officials of the investing and the host countries, as well as by observers of international affairs.

'The multinational corporation is, among other things, a private "government", often richer in assets and more populous in stockholders and employees than are some of the national states in which it carries on its business. It is simultaneously a "citizen" of several nation-states, owing obedience to their laws and paying them taxes, yet having its own objectives and being responsible to a management located in a foreign nation. Small wonder that some critics see it as an irresponsible instrument of private power or of economic "imperialism" by its own home country. Others view it as an international carrier of advanced management science and technology, an agent for the global transmission of cultures, bringing closer the day when a set of ideals will unite mankind.'[1]

While the debate about the benefits and evils of multinational business continues, it emphasizes economic success. The manager in a multinational company knows he is in a growth area of business but when he sees how it is regarded by diverse world opinion, he must ask himself how long its upward trajectory may last and whether the moral tone of its rewards is sufficiently healthy to satisfy his psychic needs. Should he stay in this business or not? And if he does, what can he do to augment its contributions and lessen its damage to the public well-being? Reading current literature on the subject should require a share of his time, but as he does so he will find that he must reach his own conclusions, because commentators of every opinion continue to walk around and peer at the multinational animal but they do not

[1] Neil H. Jacoby, 'The Multinational Corporation', *The Center Magazine*, May 1970.

147

conclude whether it should be fed or destroyed. They dispute with each other and some engage in interesting duels with themselves. They only agree that this is a big animal and growing more robust, and most of them end their analysis by walking away and muttering, 'Something has to be done to control this.' Meanwhile, new studies are launched, some of them of impressive proportions, such as the research project financed largely by the Ford Foundation and being carried out by a university team headed by Professor Raymond Vernon of the Harvard Business School. The study has already published three or four books and it is still far from presenting final conclusions. But Raymond Vernon has already concluded that 'something will have to be done' about the conflict between the interests of multinational corporations and those of the nation states.

It is imperative that the manager in the field understands the issue because, as the controversy develops, it will influence his standing in the community, it will affect his state of mind, and it may open some opportunities to be useful to his company while perhaps closing others. These pages will attempt to offer a synthesis of the debate. The more kindly procedure might be to start with some statements of support for the role of the multinational corporation. Reverting to its dispute with nation states, Arnold Toynbee dismisses the question summarily, first by extolling the benefits to society of the multinational corporation as an instrument for the transmission of technological and business knowledge, a distributor of capital and goods, and a stimulant to needy economies. He tends to discard adverse theories by pointing out that in the flow of history the nation state is a recent arrival which has not proved its value and has no sacred right to be a permanent part of human society. In fact Toynbee has real doubts about the usefulness of the nation state as it is constituted, and feels that it is on the road to being replaced by supranational political organizations.

Peter Drucker, professor at the New York University School of Business and one of the most widely-quoted business writers, comes down flatly on the side of the international company, saying:

'Its development during the last twenty years may well be the most significant event in the world economy and the one that, in the long run, will bring the greatest benefits. This institution is the "multinational" corporation [which] . . . creates a genuine economic com-

148

munity transcending national lives and yet respectful of the national sovereignties and local cultures.'

Most observers, taking an objective posture, tend to balance the benefits and disadvantages of multinational business action against each other, and then emerge at the end of the tunnel with one or more suggestions as to what should be done to resolve the contradictions. Some pit the company against the state, others judge it against the needs of the developing world, and a few look at it from the standpoint of its country of origin. Jan van Ommen of Unilever, in a talk to a business group, has taken the historical perspective.

Van Ommen pointed out that in the nineteenth century the United States, Australia, New Zealand (he might have added Canada and Japan) were developing countries and that in the early stages of their growth they benefited immensely from a foreign injection of capital and skills brought by multinational interests centred in the more advanced nations. He believes that a similar process can likewise spur the new crop of developing nations. He is aware, however, that these nations are critical of multinational corporations for a number of reasons, some of which we list here with our comments:

1. Adversaries contend that multinational corporations too often demand or seek protected monopoly positions. They point to the geographical distribution of oil and mining concessions and such deals as the Peron government's pledge to maintain a five-year import barrier to protect Squibb's investment in the installation of a penicillin plant.

The multinationals reply that the only occasions when they aspire to monopoly situations, except by virtue of producing superior products or services, occur when they accept high-risk situations or a monopoly incentive is offered to them. In less-developed countries where home industries enjoy tariff protection, they seek nothing more than the same protection. When these markets are too small to support more than one industry in a certain field, the foreign investor does not want to see competition create an unfeasible economic situation. When a developing country offers the incentive of protection, the foreign company will not refuse it.

2. It is contended that foreign direct investors do not accede to local

149

planning priorities. They may locate plants where they are least desired (by the planners), they may draw off labour needed for other national purposes, and their export performance may fall short of the country's effort to obtain foreign exchange. Also, they may counter financial policies by seeking local financing instead of bringing in funds for investment and growth

The multinationals state that they follow rules already established when they enter the market and cannot easily change plant locations or labour sources as national plans are altered. Their export performance depends in large part on costs of production which often, by virtue of local regulations, are too high to permit the export rate they would like to establish. They also point out that local finance is available to their local competitors and their rights in the matter should be equal. However, they contend that their operations develop funding, much of which they reinvest in the host country.

3. Officials point out that multinational guests are a constant threat to a country's economy because they may withdraw if their operations are unprofitable, thereby causing damage to labour, creditors, and local investors.

The guest companies admit that their responsibilities to their stockholders take precedence over commitments in host countries. They claim that their record is generally good in maintaining operations abroad where commitments have been made, unless local state harassment or a collapse in local economic conditions makes profitable operations impossible or unlikely. Their contention may become subject to further challenge with the enlargement and integration of the Common Market, for many firms who established plants in each of the EEC countries may decide to rationalize their production operations, thereby shutting down plants in various locations for their own purposes. Officials continue to be concerned over the negative power of the multinational, pointing to past plant closures and to occasions when the decision of an international company not to enter a market with production facilities has been considered damaging – as when an American automobile producer decided to build a plant in Belgium instead of France and when Henry Ford announced in the U.K. that his company would not invest further in Britain because of labour instability.

4. Countries claim that foreign investors create planning problems by clustering plants in the areas most favoured by industry, leaving the rest of the country relatively underdeveloped.

The guest companies say that they are doing no more nor less than local industry while insisting that they are more responsive to government inducements to set up operations in special areas. They give as evidence the foreign plants in development areas of the U.K., the responses of multinational companies to French and Belgian incentives for industrialization of neglected regions, and their favourable reactions to the incentives offered by needy states like Puerto Rico and Ireland.

5. Critics contend that the overseas subsidiaries of international companies cause a drain on their exchange reserves through their withdrawals for dividend payments, royalties, and a high rate of profit remittance to their home offices.

The extractive industries are hard put to answer this charge because they usually withdraw the product – crude oil and ore – and the profits as well. They do contend that their creation of these industries has poured wealth into the host countries, as in the Middle East, but that it has been mismanaged in most cases. In the Middle East they have offered, with mild success, their advisory services on the local use of oil wealth, but have not been able to establish a consultant relationship in Chile.

The multinational manufacturers' defence is that they create capital accumulation by advancing local industry and by virtue of their exports, which bring in more exchange than they take out. Authorities in the U.K., for example, admit that American companies established there have helped build exchange reserves through their export operations. In the less-developed countries the point is harder to make. Manufactured products in these countries cannot usually face price competition on the world market, especially products from Latin America and Africa. However these products, it is stated, often save exchange by providing a local substitution for products which might otherwise have to be imported.

The issue is difficult to generalize, as conditions in the various countries, regions, and industries vary so greatly. The situation is becoming even more confused as American multinationals answer the charges of their domestic labour leaders and politicians that their operations abroad are adding to the U.S. exchange deficit, with surveys showing that they are bringing home more dollars than they export. How these companies are going to convince both the parent country and the host countries that they add to positive exchange balances for both will be an interesting exercise.

Mr van Ommen sets against the criticisms of multinational operators a few of the points made in their favour. He states that in many cases the multinational company, and only the multinational company, can marshal the combination of assets required to establish a new enterprise in a country which may need it. He draws on business history to demonstrate that generally such an industry is a long-term investment and that the multinational company usually has the necessary access to long-term loans to keep it on the rails. He also draws attention to the ability of the multinational firm to quickly bring into a market the benefits of research long-financed by the parent company. Here he moves over controversial ground, for many critics argue that the tendency of such companies to keep their research operations at home denies a facility which could greatly benefit the host country. As his final argument for the multinational company, Jan van Ommen cites the constellation effect which the new enterprise introduces, its attraction of complementary businesses to the host country in the form of suppliers of raw and semiprocessed materials and purveyors of complementary services. He sees no insurmountable barrier to satisfactory relationships between the company and the host country, stating only in the case of the less-developed countries that they would be better able to enjoy the benefits of international business if they reduced their tariff agreements with their neighbours to create larger regional markets. The case in point, of course, is the Common Market and the beneficial exploitation of its opportunities by cross-border firms.

One of the most articulate and assiduous students of multinational business problems, Jack N. Behrman, has summed up the pros and cons of the multinational firm in its confrontation with nation states, in his book *National Interests and the Multinational Enterprise*. Some of the issues duplicate those cited by Jan van Ommen but there are others of significant importance.

In favour of the multinational company, Behrman agrees that it makes a contribution to capital formation in a host country, bringing in and organizing capital to generate local profits, and earning foreign exchange through its exports. He is fully aware of the arguments for and against this assertion, noting that in Europe an important side effect has been the creation of a Eurocurrency, and that another has been to help make available the liquidity necessary for expanding world trade. And in spite of the complaints of less-developed countries that the capital formation contributed is later cancelled out by exchange withdrawals, he believes the benefit is a positive one.

Another contribution cited by Behrman is the transfer of technology by multinational firms. Most observers agree on this, realizing that the success of the multinational company abroad depends largely upon its ability to bring new technology into foreign markets which are enriched by the new knowledge available to them.

Likewise, and there is little dispute on this point, the companies bring with them management skills which not only stay in the host country but which are diffused by the personnel training procedures of the companies which transfer them. In fact, as has been noted, in some areas the companies are troubled by the tendency of local firms to poach the multinational's newly trained local men, obtaining the benefits of the imported management skills at the expense of the multinational enterprise.

Behrman also discusses the economic development which international companies bring to depressed areas. The best evidence that this is tangible and desirable is the widespread offering of incentives by governments to attract foreign investment to these areas.

The competitive stimulus that the guest companies bring to some national economies is accepted as a healthy prod to laggard local business. This is not so often the case in a less-developed economy, but it has been observed that in countries like France and Britain the old family-owned firms have often tried to modernize their methods when challenged by skilled intruders. In many cases the value of this stimulus has been certified by the willingness of some of the older local companies to merge with new multinationals who enter the arena.

Behrman also confirms that the multinationals make a positive contribution to the host country's economy by producing exportable products which earn foreign exchange.

In his discussion Behrman reinforces the assumption that the nation states accept the above list of benefits conferred by multinational companies. The nations desire the reinforcement of their economies by new infusions of capital, technology, and management skills. They welcome aid to their depressed areas and are grateful for the strengthening of their foreign exchange position. These benefits are considered desirable – if they could be controlled. But most countries harbour a resentment of companies operating on their territory whose policies are formed and whose major decisions are made outside their borders in the companies' home offices. Behrman makes little point of this resentment, unlike many other observers, but he does elaborate on the ancillary complaints.

One among them is that the multinational firm often achieves dominance in the field of particular industries. A prime example is IBM with its leadership almost everywhere in the world that it operates. Aware of its power and of the wish of host governments that their own computer industries might match or surpass it, IBM is careful to fragment its manufacturing process wherever a regional arrangement like the EEC or LAFTA will allow it to bring the pieces together across borders. The takeover of most of the German petroleum market by foreign companies is another example, one which suddenly aroused German authorities to strongly object to further inroads.

Another fear of government authorities, paradoxically, concerns technology. They look with dismay on their country's growing dependence on multinational companies for expanding areas of technology within their borders. They want the technology brought in, they desire its healthy growth locally, but they hate to become dependent on it if it belongs to foreigners who could withdraw it.

The same sort of attitude appears in the statement of local critics that the foreign companies can disturb their government's economic plans. No very convincing examples are offered of companies which have actually upset the economic planning of a nation state, but the conviction is expressed that the giant companies may have the power to do so. It is, therefore, the potential rather than the actuality which is feared. Some of this fear arises from the original irritation of officials over the fact that the subsidiaries which are guests in their country will respond to orders from the home office rather than to the dictates of the host government. In France long-term planning is jointly carried out by government and industry leaders. But the French government cannot sit down with a board of directors or chief operating officer

154

located in New York, London or Amsterdam. Understandably this causes the government some feelings of frustration and irritation.

The fears of governments on this issue are not entirely without basis. Although no cases of companies purposely contravening a country's economic plan have been publicized, there have been and are occasions when multinational action responds to its own interests without much regard for the interests of the host countries. Perhaps the most flamboyant of such actions occur when a revaluation appears imminent – as when multinational cash flowed into Germany to accelerate the revaluation of the Deutschmark and earlier, when companies weakened the pound by financial transfers to cover their cash exposure. Financial manipulations of this sort do oppose short-term national planning. Also, the use of transfer pricing to bring in raw materials at high prices for processing in a tax-high country or one otherwise trying to protect its exchange reserves, is not unknown. And finally, the denial of an export market to a foreign subsidiary because it is the terrain of the parent company or another subsidiary hinders the export programme of the host country concerned. In these cases actuality and potential too often converge.

Again, it is the potential of the multinational company which concerns governments when they consider that a growing part of their nation's technology and export trade is in the hands of foreigners. Examples of bad behaviour on the part of the companies are rarely cited but the potential may exist and governments are increasingly aware of it as a challenge to their economic security.

A final source of dissatisfaction concerns the American companies because of their government's assertion of the right to extend its anti-trust regulatory powers wherever the American multinationals operate. This extraterritorial intrusion into the economic pattern of other states is, not unreasonably, resented by the companies as well as their host governments. Actuality has proved the potential in this case, with the forced break-up of the old Dupont-ICI agreement and the re-partition of Esso-Socony world markets demanded by the U.S. government.

Anthony Wedgwood Benn, a leading member of the British Labour Party and shadow minister for Trade and Industry, reflected a nation state point of view in the following statement made at a closed round-table meeting of international executives in January 1972:

155

'Multinational enterprises have therefore got to face the fact that they are in politics – whether they like it or not. The greatest mistake they can make is to think of themselves purely in business terms, or to suppose that the fact that they operate internationally makes them, in some way, morally virtuous as internationalists standing against the nation state. For the nation state at present offers the only scope for popular influence to be brought to bear on the political and economic power of business.

'. . . The first concern of governments in dealing with multinational enterprise lies in the area of industrial and economic policy where the multinational corporation has a built-in advantage deriving from its international status, permitting it to escape more easily from domestic legislation of all kinds by planning its own development in a way that best suits its own interest, undertaking new investment to take advantage of lower labour costs, lower taxation, and easier labour relations and to avoid domestic regulations governing pollution or measures to locate industry to meet the regional policy of national government.'

Mr Wedgwood Benn's comments, politically oriented as they well might be, tend to represent the home country rather than the host government and they reflect an organized-labour viewpoint. It is not surprising that he should worry over the multinational firm's ability to evade the dictates of its own government on certain matters, simply by choosing in many cases to export its operations to a friendlier climate. In so doing, it may also offend organized labour, as Mr Wedgwood Benn has hinted. The American AFL-CIO has presented its case against American multinationals to Congress and demanded that they should be curbed. It also requested tariff protection for local industry.

American labour union statisticians state that 74 per cent of U.S. imports in 1966 could have been produced domestically, which would have created 1·9 million jobs. In 1968, the estimate was 2·4 million jobs. Labour leaders also accuse American companies of closing down jobs by setting up satellite plants to produce the more labour-intensive product components abroad, and then bringing the semifinished product to the United States for final processing.

The motivation of multinational firms in establishing manufacturing facilities abroad is challenged not only by their home labour unions but by many of the countries that receive them. More and more informed sectors of the younger generation in the less-developed countries claim that the foreign companies, which their governments have welcomed, are simply exporting pollution while exploiting their low-paid working class. This threatens to become the next phase of resentment in these countries. The dilemma of the multinational firms in dealing with the less-developed countries is shared with the governments of developed countries in their aid programmes. Tibor Mende, writer of *From Aid to Recolonization: the Story of a Failure*, and a leading authority on North-South geopolitics maintains that government or business relationships with the less-developed countries are built on quicksand. In both cases, for government and business, the arrangements are made with governments which do not represent their people. The military governments of Latin America, the one-man states in Africa, and the minority democracies in Latin America and South-East Asia impose upon their people regimes which do not have their support or consent. Therefore an emotional hostility exists towards the multinational companies which are guests by invitation of these governments.

This builds an aspect of vulnerability into the relationship. The government of a less-developed country, acting for itself or for hostile local business leaders, can take action against the multinational guest knowing that in this policy at least it will be supported by the mass of its people. It may even take such aggressive action to win a measure of popular support. Many a minor dictator has publicly declaimed against the foreign intruder while privately making a profitable deal with a new guest. Finally he has had to make good his bombast by expropriating the local assets of one company or another.

An article by *Fortune* magazine moves the background for appraisal of multinational business action back to the developed countries. In doing so it reminds us of the companies who operate in both worlds and raises the question of how a company can have one 'good corporate citizen' policy for forty different countries.

Fortune's summary of the pros and cons states:

'A nation does pay a price when part of its industry is controlled from outside. It may lose tax revenues because the corporation is manipulating transfer prices between subsidiaries. When the multinational corporation uses its financial network to pull money out of a country in balance-of-payments trouble or to move money into one struggling to damp-down inflation, the government rightfully feels that it is losing control over the domestic economy. And when a company like Massey-Ferguson uses its international flexibility to reroute a subsidiary's purchases through Britain rather than France the move may mean a sudden drop in French exports.

'The global company may upset an economy by pulling out entirely. Clearly many companies invested in Europe during the early days of the EEC. Since the elimination of trade barriers was then very much in the future, they put down too many plants in too many locations. Now both objective conditions and managerial sophistication will suggest a consolidation of facilities. A country will naturally worry that its plant may be rationalized away.

'Arrayed against this partial list of costs, however, is an impressive tally of benefits. By building plants and sometimes starting wholly new industries, multinational corporations increase output and expand tax revenues. They upgrade local labour and management and they provide consumers with more efficiently made and better-serviced products. Often improved labour relations can be added to the list, especially where U.S.-based companies are concerned. This is hard to pin down precisely but it is significant that IBM French workers did not participate in the strike last spring.'[2]

Although the debate continues it does not move far from the ground we have just covered. Too often the adversaries state their case in general terms and leave the impression that a multinational company's vices and virtues are the same wherever it may operate, with some general distinctions between its relationships with developed and less-developed countries. The disputants overlook the variety in types of industries, companies, and nations, and well they might until business scholars find the time to assemble data on the entire panorama of global business, which may well be the goal of Professor Raymond Vernon and his Ford Foundation-Harvard Business School project. If so, they may encounter situations where a single company meets the stresses of nearly all the diverse relationships possible.

Let us suppose, for example, that a petroleum company operates worldwide. Some do. It takes the raw product out of the ground in one

[2] *Fortune*, September 15, 1968.

or more Middle Eastern or Latin American countries. Its concessions may well have been taken over in at least one of those countries. The others are engaged in continual dispute with their concessionaires and the company is the object of emotional hostility from a variety of people whose totalitarian leaders fan the fire for negotiating purposes. The company is bartering for concessions in other such territories, where the story may be repeated.

It refines the products nearer to its major market, let us say the European area. In relation to gasoline marketing it meets free-enterprise competition in some nations and must compete with state-owned oil marketers in France, Italy, and Spain, where it is grudgingly allowed a quota of the market. Its marketing activities include, however, some of the Latin American countries which are also its sources for crude oil, and here government regulations and threats of reduced market quotas are a fact of life. Finally, seeking the posture of corporate good citizen, the company manufactures fertilizers as a petroleum derivative and offers them with agricultural services to the less-developed countries. Some accept the offer but do not relinquish their hostility. Others, like India, welcome the fertilizer and the accompanying services as a social contribution.

Policy is shaped in the home office but against such a patchwork background of the company's global operations – and here they have been sketched all too briefly – the inputs of regional and country managers in the field are a continuing necessity. The manager abroad is not only an operating resource but, as an informant, must be a contributing policy-maker.

Government reactions. In this phase of his role the manager abroad must inform himself about the reactions of the two sides: how governments respond to the pressures they feel from the multinational companies and how the companies react to government attitudes and measures. As the *International Labour Review* has stated: 'Managers are influential agents of social changes ... are the first to contact new ideas ... can spread them ... and should be aware of the influence they can exert.'[3]

Government reactions vary according to ideology and the economic situation, as well as to the historical forces that shape their thinking.

[3] *International Labour Review*, August 1966.

Some severely restrict the freedom of multinational companies to join their economies. Postwar Japan, reaching back to its history of complete isolation from the Western world and forward to its status as a destroyed country, placed tight restraints on direct foreign investment within its borders.

This policy was in place during its years of surging growth, and Japan maintained it even when it had become one of the world's leading economic powers. The demands of other nations for liberalization of Japan's attitude toward direct foreign investment brought some softening of its restrictions, if not of its attitude. Foreign companies can now join Japanese firms in certain circumstances, but must accept minority positions. On occasion foreign companies have been able to enter the country to help satisfy needs that might be difficult to supply without them, but they have been closely controlled as to remittance of profits.

France retains the right to screen proposals for direct investment from abroad. British official agencies have been known to disapprove foreign takeovers of English firms and the German government not long ago remonstrated against absorption of a local petroleum marketing organization. The AMCON countries of the Andean region have ruled that foreign companies may operate only by phasing in local ownership to an eventual majority position in foreign subsidiaries in that region. Mexico has long kept a tight rein on foreign companies, requiring that they share equity with local capital, include Mexicans in their management, and over a period of time increase in their products the percentage of components made in Mexico. Yet Mexico is not hostile to foreign investment *per se* if it meets the nation's requirements, as the following 1971 Mexican government decree demonstrates:

'A presidential decree published in today's issue of the Official Gazette grants tax and other incentives to those companies which are formed or expanded for the purpose of promoting regional development, substituting imports, increasing exports, creating new jobs and assisting in improving the balance of payments of the country.

'These incentives, which will be set forth in general rules, will be allowed irrespective of the fact that companies may already or in the future be entitled to tax incentives under other federal provisions.

'For this purpose an interministerial committee composed by the

Ministries of Finance and Industry and Commerce has been formed. In determining the nature and extent of the incentives this committee will take into account the following factors:

(*a*) The characteristics of the geographic zone or region of the country in which the company will operate.

(*b*) Its contribution to the industrial production and integration and to the development of the region.

(*c*) The type of industrial activity.

(*d*) The creation of new jobs.

(*e*) The prices and quality of the items which will be produced as well as the national content of said items.

(*f*) The effects of its transactions on the country's balance of payments.

(*g*) Its capital structure.

(*h*) Other concurring circumstances.

'The incentives may also be granted to companies which are already established if by doing so they will rationalize their production and increase their efficiency and productivity and thus benefit national consumers and increase their exports.'

Mexico, as opposed to Japan, encourages joint ventures, but under a set of rules guaranteeing local partners major participation in the investment and its operation. Other governments, in varying degree, concur with the Mexican policy. Among the newcomers in this respect is Yugoslavia, which now allows foreign companies to join with local state-controlled companies. The issue of joint ventures is a crucial one. Most multinational companies try to avoid them because they do not feel that their local national partners can assimilate the company's global point of view and will thus reduce the subsidiary's freedom in such matters as export policy, declaration or withholding of dividends, reinvestment, and diversification. Regardless, and because governments may want to restrict foreign companies' free choice in such operations, many of them make it difficult to enter their domains without taking a local partner. The restriction, rarely if ever written into law, is more common among the less-developed countries.

Another restriction on the expansion of the multinationals is the

161

existence in many countries of state-owned companies which enjoy certain privileges in competing with foreign guests. The less-developed countries all seek to own an airline and a steel mill, and some a petroleum exploration and marketing company, but few can afford to operate other businesses. However, we do find INI in Spain, a government conglomerate; ENI in Italy, in a variety of businesses; government financing in companies in France and England and, of course, the state-owned companies of Eastern Europe. By quota limitation, privilege, or direct mandate, these companies keep their share of the domestic economy relatively free of foreign incursion.

Another state defence, or offence, against foreign companies is the highly publicized act of expropriation. The extractive industries and the public utilities are the most common victims of this response to their presence, and the Latin American and North African countries rely on it most frequently. One can expect expropriation in the future to occur in other African and possibly South-East Asian countries when the investments become sufficiently tempting. The threat of expropriation has become so widespread and the losses so costly that the multinational extractive industries are reviewing means of countering them. Some see promise in a version of the arrangements usually made by Hilton Hotels abroad, wherein local sources put up most of the capital and Hilton accepts a service contract allowing it a share of the profits. The problem, of course, is to find sufficient local capital.

According to one report, Gordon Murphy, new president of the copper-mining Cerro Corporation, contends that the extractive industries will have to come to some such arrangement with national governments. Murphy has said: 'Without capital the drive of people for better living cannot be achieved. And if they can't get control by other means, they will have no alternative but confiscation.' Cerro went into a joint venture with the Chilean government but the issue is still in doubt.

'So far as we know,' said Murphy, 'we were the first company to develop property from scratch with the host country as an equity partner.'[4] He went on to describe a scheme for mining companies that would be based on an agreed timetable for turning over control to the host government after a period of years if the compensation to the company could be fairly stated.

[4] *Business Week*, September 12, 1970.

Looming over the scene is the likelihood of eventual supra-government confrontation with the multinationals. In fact most proposals for adjustment of the relationships between the international companies and nation states, as we shall see, fall into this area. Students of the subject have already noted how Common Market regulations affect cross-border operations in the area. The EEC Commission's rules on cartels, pollution control and product quality are some of the measures which apply to international and national companies alike. The structure of AMCON in South America is primarily a protective mechanism concerning foreign investment in the Andean region. These are only among the latest of collective government efforts to control multinational companies. Other joint efforts, of both commercial and government organizations, have a history of some decades. Agreements and proposals have included:

The International Code of Fair Treatment for Foreign Investments drawn up by the International Chamber of Commerce Committees on Foreign Investments and Foreign Establishments and approved by the ICC's Quebec Congress in June 1949;

The Economic Agreement of Bogota, 1948;

Some Guiding Principles of Good Corporate Behaviour for Subsidiaries of Foreign Companies in Canada, suggested by the Canadian Department of Trade and Commerce, 1967;

Precepts for Successful Business Operations Procedures of Foreign Companies in Canada, suggested by the Canadian Department of Trade and Commerce, 1967;

Precepts for Successful Business Operations Procedures in Canada and the United States, Canada-United States Committee;

Summary recommendations of the Stikker Report on the Role of Private Enterprise in Investment and Promotion of Exports in Developing Countries, United Nations, 1968;

Pacific Basin Charter on International Investment, 1971.

On the side of business, responses to government hostility have varied according to the company. Other than the efforts of the International Chamber of Commerce there have been few examples of joint company action. Perhaps most notable in recent years has been the

163

negotiations of a loose association of petroleum companies with the petroleum-producing states. So far these have been confined to discussions about the product's price and consideration of the states' demands for equity shares of the companies. Eventually these contacts may shape a code of conduct.

On other occasions companies have sought the support of their home governments, as in the notorious ITT case and previously when American oil companies were expropriated by the Mexican and Peruvian governments. However, governments have been loath to return to the days of the gunboat, and this type of company reaction does not even aspire to be constructive.

The more positive company thrusts toward healthy relationships with nation states are based on new attitudes. There is a greater recognition that apart from commercial considerations, a company should bring something new with it when it crosses foreign borders. Its contribution should be a better product, better services, an exportable product which will shore up the nation's balance of payments, or one which achieves the same goal by substituting for a formerly imported product. There is increasing recognition that short-term planning depends too heavily on quick recovery of investment through excessively high profits and remittances, which may make a company either redundant or a burden on the country's economy. There is some acceptance of the fact that a company's security abroad is enhanced by its ability to continually produce something which the country itself might otherwise do without or be forced to import. Some companies have realized that installing research and development facilities abroad makes them more desirable guests and opens new sources of creative participation. Others, dealing with less-developed countries, are exploring the possibilities of tailoring their research to the needs of the local economy rather than imposing their own product concepts on populations not ready for them. And as we have mentioned, the idea of service contracts associated with local national capital, as exemplified by the Hilton Hotel chain, is taking hold. It is also increasingly apparent that every country will appreciate the contribution of foreign companies who make conscientious efforts to raise the level of national working and management competence through local training programmes. The managers abroad have often been the chief motivators in setting up these programmes, individually within the companies and jointly with other firms in the area. Generally, workforce training is an in-plant activity. Management training varies but increasingly it is coming to include the support of independent local management-education institutions as they may appear.

Business has been particularly responsive to the aims and potential benefits of regional government associations. It has been repeatedly observed that the American companies were quick to stimulate the prosperity of the Common Market, and therefore their own, by operating within its area. The European multinational companies have not been slow to follow them and increasingly European national companies are coming to realize the value of cross-border operations, adding their reinforcement to the Common Market concept. Meanwhile the Americans have encouraged the South American countries to push ahead with LAFTA and the Central American Common Market. In all these cases, expanding the regional market potential to accommodate the production of the giant companies is their major aim, but an ancillary result of equal importance is the co-ordination of governments in dealing with the giant companies.

As business and government warily seek to co-ordinate their interests they increasingly find that they are treading firm ground in their efforts. Arnold Toynbee may pronounce the nation state an anachronism, but no businessman will agree with him. Strong stable governments are desirable for the growth of multinational business just as expanding commercial activity is a prerequisite for political stability. True, some social philosophers now challenge the validity of growth in production, claiming that zero production growth will provide the only opportunity to save the social and physical environment, but the likelihood is that their challenge will at most result in agreement to redirect the trends of growth rather than stifle them. Multinational business rightfully claims that the three prerequisite conditions for its prosperity are peace, free trade, and trained men, and governments cannot but concur in the advantages of these requirements. The multinational transfers of products, technology, and skills cannot take place where war prevails, neither can they flow at the optimum pace where trade barriers exist. To effect these transfers and make them flourish, trained men are needed. Governments cannot responsibly take an opposing view, even those which erect barriers to protect their national ideologies and industries.

165

Proposals. Considering the depth and breadth of the debate concerning the stance of multinational business and the nation states, remarkably few impressive proposals for improving it have been offered. More and more are being advanced, however, and as each comes forward there is usually something new entangled in the rhetoric, providing hope that bringing together the best of the current thinking will cause a breakthrough.

Neil Jacoby emphasizes the joint responsibility of governments and suggests that an agency like the United Nations might eventually shelter and control multinational business for the common good. He contends that a solution is urgent because:

'The multinational corporation is, beyond doubt, the most powerful agency for regional and global economic unity that our century has produced. It is fundamentally an instrument of peace. Its transactions are transnational in nature and purpose. Its interest is to emphasize the common goals of peoples, to reconcile or remove differences between them. It cannot thrive in a regime of international tension and conflict. Is it too much to hope that, through the instrumentality of multinational business, the imperatives of world economic progress will ultimately succeed in doing what the awful threat of nuclear destruction has so far failed to accomplish – to bring unity to mankind?'[5]

Jacoby's proposals also include a set of commandments for the company. They stress the need for effective communication with communities abroad, identification with those communities, conformity with their business practices, advancement of their local employees in the foreign subsidiaries, establishment of local research and development units and, important to the manager abroad, maximum decentralization and delegation of authority to managers of foreign affiliates.

Other proponents of joint government co-ordination to deal with multinational business are numerous. Raymond Vernon is among them. *The Economist* has reported on this group as against those who seek purely national solutions. At a meeting of multinational businessmen and public leaders, Anthony Wedgwood Benn has been more explicit.

'The necessary framework within which global corporations should operate,' he stated, 'will have to be constructed at various levels from the United Nations right down to the plant level.

[5] Jacoby, *op. cit.*

'The internationalization of industrial technology has now proceeded so rapidly that it is not unreasonable to expect that the UN – set up to prevent the misuses of military technology by war – should extend its functions to take on board responsibility for supervising some aspects of the operation of global companies that are of international concern.

'What may well be required is something approaching the diplomatic recognition of these companies, when they reach a certain size, holding them accountable directly to the UN for any of their decisions that affect international peace and security or human rights . . .'

At the same meeting, one organized by the Business International Corporation, Eldridge Haynes, chairman of that firm, suggested that the international establishment to which companies should respond would best be organized by themselves. In describing this proposed entity, Mr Haynes declared:

'While openly sponsored and supported by multinational corporations – who are its members – I visualize a board of trustees of the proposed organization composed of distinguished internationally-oriented and dedicated business, labour, political, academic and church leaders from many countries. It should be made indelibly clear to everyone that this is an *international* organization, and not one organized to benefit people in a particular country – or to serve as an instrument of any nation state. It should be equally clear that this new organization is sincerely dedicated to the principle that what is best for humanity is best for the multinational corporation . . .'

Research, a continuing dialogue between members, and close co-operation with the United Nations, would constitute the framework of action for such an organization, according to Mr Haynes.

Mr Haynes' proposal might well be taken seriously, as the time approaches when the multinational companies may seek each other's company for protection. For protection against what? In a sense a multinational company is only a national firm which has outgrown its own country's market and the difference between the international and the national enterprise is that the former deals in a variety of the world's markets and the latter operates in the one at home. However, another difference is fundamental enough to affect the survival of the

167

multinational firm. Whereas the multinational company is often feared by host governments because its home office is not responsible to them, the multinational itself is equally apprehensive of those governments because they have no constitutional responsibility towards the visitor. At home its employees, suppliers and customers can vote or otherwise apply legitimate pressure on the authorities. Abroad its citizenship is only titular. It is far different to be a voting citizen at home than an honorary one abroad. At home its managers can admonish their parliamentary or congressional representatives; overseas the managers can attempt to develop influence but can hardly aspire to political power. The job of the manager abroad requires more adroitness because he lacks the political leverage he has in his home country.

Whether or not the company's home government alters the value of its currency is a matter in which the company's intervention is influential. Abroad it has no voice in the matter but may suffer drastically from the consequences. At home the stability of the government is a condition which can be affected by local business; abroad it has no say in the matter of government succession. At home the company can protest against the incursion of the government into business; abroad it must maintain a discreet silence. At home the company's views help form public opinion on the question of free trade; abroad it must accept trade protectionism that limits the flow of trade, hoping only that its home government will exert pressures against this policy. At home the company can follow a single pattern of policies regarding its commercial and social position; abroad its policies vary with the countries in which it operates and the type of business it does in each. The manager abroad, then, has the dual responsibility of contributing to the formation of the firm's global policy as well as the one to be applied in the subsidiary under his administration. It is no wonder that multinational firms favour the formation of regional markets and hope that each will diminish the fragmentation of official attitudes in the area. The manager abroad, in his contacts with local business and local officials, can further the concept of regionalization, as many have in Latin America and Europe.

The relationship of the multinational firm with local populations overseas contains the same dispute concerning its social responsibilities as is found in the home office's country. Concern with ecology has become universal. The EEC Commission's environmental programme reaches all companies operating within the region but it also affects those that export to the Common Market because it will include product safety standards for all goods sold in the region. It will deal with disparities between national regulations governing the composition of goods, such as lead in gasoline and additives in foods, and it will attempt to bring together the various laws on pollution control. One aspect on which all governments appear to be in agreement is that the cost of such control will have to be borne by the polluter, e.g. the manufacturer. Some industries are taking joint action to respond to public demand. A number of petroleum companies have created a common fund in London to meet the expenses of oil spills. Paper makers in the U.S., Canada, Norway, Finland, and Sweden are planning to exchange knowledge and co-ordinate efforts to develop pollution controls in their industry.

The multinational companies are distributing the benefits of transfers of their capital and skills from country to country. They proclaim the desire to achieve the status of good citizens wherever they may be, but citizenship is an empty word when they are not constitutionally citizens. The closest they can come to it is to study the aspirations of people wherever they may be, in wealthy countries or poor, north, south or at home, and then to evaluate their operations so as to eliminate those practices that harm public welfare and install those that can enrich it. The co-ordination of such policies can be accomplished in the home office boardrooms, but the input that will make them responsive to populations abroad and the implementation that will make them effective must rest with the subsidiary managers abroad, and to them should be delegated the authority to do the job, for society everywhere will settle for nothing less.

Select Bibliography

BOOKS

Behrman, Jack N., *National Interests and the Multinational Enterprise,* Englewood Cliffs: Prentice-Hall, 1970.

Brooke, M. & Remmers, H. L., *The Strategy of International Enterprise*, London: Longman, 1970.

Ewing, J. & Meissner, F., *International Business Management*, California: Wadsworth, 1964.

Kindleberger, Charles P., *Power and Money*, New York and London: Basic Books Inc., 1970.

——, *The International Corporation*, Cambridge and London: Massachusetts Institute of Technology Press, 1970.

Robinson, Richard D., *International Management*, New York: Holt, Rhinehart & Winston, 1967.

Stonehill, A., *International Financial Management*, California: Goodyear Publishing Co., 1970.

Tinbergen, Jan, *Shaping the World Economy*, New York: The Twentieth Century Fund, 1962.

JOURNALS

Bettignies & Rhinesmith, 'Developing the International Executive', *European Business* (Paris), Summer 1970.

Buzzell, Robert D., 'Can You Standardize Multinational Marketing?', *Harvard Business Review*, November–December 1968.

Davis, Stanley M., 'U.S. versus Latin America: Business and Culture', *Harvard Business Review* (Cambridge), December 1969.

Haider, M., 'Tomorrow's Executive: A Man for All Countries', *Columbia Journal of World Business*, Winter 1966.

Heenan, David A., 'The Corporate Expatriate: Assignment to Ambiguity', *Columbia Journal of World Business*, May–June 1970.

Holton, Richard H., 'Marketing Policies in Multinational Corporations', *California Management Review*, Summer 1971.

Jacoby, Neil H., 'The Multinational Corporation', *The Center Magazine*, May 1970.

Knortz, Herbert C., 'The Job of the International Financial Manager', *Management Review*, September 1969.

Kolde, Endel J. & Hill, Richard E., 'Conceptual and Normative Aspects of International Management', *Academy of Management Journal*, June 1967.

Kotler, Philip, 'Coping with the Complexities of Marketing', *The Conference Board Record*, January 1969.

Newman, William H., 'Is Management Exportable?', *Columbia Journal of World Business*, January–February 1970.

Reddig, William M., 'The New Multinational Manager', American Management Association, *Management Review*, February 1970.

Shetty, Y. K., 'International Manager: A Role Profile', *Management International Review*, April–May 1971.

Sweeney, James K., 'A Small Company Enters the European Market', *Harvard Business Review*, September–October 1970.

Teague, Frederick A., 'International Management Selection and Development', *California Management Review*, Spring 1970.

Thomas, Doina, 'The Continental', London: *Management Today*, December 1969.

Tookey, Douglas, 'International Business and Political Geography', *British Journal of Marketing*, Autumn 1969.

Vernon, Raymond, 'The Multinational Enterprise: Power vs. Sovereignty', New York, *Foreign Affairs*, July 1971.

Wanger, Shelley, 'Multinational Advertising Takes Off', *Vision*, February 15, 1972.

'World Business Series', *Harvard Business Review*, Parts I and II, 1954–64.

International Labour Review (Geneva), August 1966.

'What it Takes to Work Abroad', *International Management*, London, October 1970.

'Firms Begin to Train Managers for Abroad', *International Management*, London, October 1970.

'Multinational Business', *The Economist*, London, January 22, 1972.

Report of *The Economist* Intelligence Unit, London, October 1969.

PAPERS

Adderley, H. A., 'The Psychology of the Expatriate Manager', for the Centre d'Etudes Industrielles, Geneva.

Behrman, Jack N., 'The Multinational Enterprise and Economic Integration'.

Clee, Gilbert H., 'The Emerging World Enterprise'.

Haynes, Eldridge, 'Collective Action by Multinational Corporations – a Proposal'.

Ramel, Stig. 'Sweden Today'.

Vernon, Raymond, 'Economic Sovereignty at Bay'.

——, 'Problems and Prospects for the Multinational Enterprise'.

——, 'Thinking Ahead'.

Van Ommen, Jan, 'To the Dutch National Advisory Council on Developing Countries'.

SELECT BIBLIOGRAPHY

RESEARCH STUDIES

Business International Corporation:
  '1985/Corporate Planning Today for Tomorrow's World Market', New
    York, 1967.
  'Nationalism in Latin America', New York, 1970.
  'Decision Making in International Operations', *100 Checklists*, New York,
    1970.
  'Organizing for Latin American Operations', New York, 1969.
  'Solving International Accounting Problems', New York, 1969.
  'Solving Latin American Business Problems', New York, 1968.
Chorofas, Dimitri, 'Developing the International Executive', American
  Management Association, RS 83.
——, 'The Communications Barrier', American Management Association,
  1969.
'Foreign Nationals in International Management', National Industrial
  Conference Board, 1968.
'The Changing Role of the International Executive', National Industrial
  Conference Board, 1966.

PERIODICALS AND DAILIES

Business Europe Weekly Report.
Business International Weekly Report.
International Herald Tribune.
Journal de Genève.
Financial Times (London).
The Sunday Times (London).

Index

AFL-CIO 114, 156
Abex (U.S.A.) 65
accounting 73–86
administration 55–72
advertising 46–7, 92, 96–101; slogans 97; on television 47
American Standard 62
Argentina 41–2, 67–8; trade unions 108
Atlas Copco (Sweden) 64
attitudes to labour relations 105
automobile industry 117–18
autonomy: manufacturing 31; technical 35
Avon Products 100

Beecham Group 49
Belgium, trade unions 107
Brannen, Ted, and Frank Hodgson *Overseas Management* 120
Brazil 48; trade unions 108
Britain 49; labour relations 118
Brooke, Michael, and Lee Remmers *The Strategy of Multinational Enterprise* 39–40
business and governments 143–4, 157, 159–69
Business International *Corporate Planning Today for Tomorrow's World Market* 51–4
business schools 140–1

Campbell Soup 47
cash management 80–1
centralization and decentralization 55–72; in marketing 87
Coca-Cola 48, 94, 97, 100
communications 60–5; among managers 141–2; financial 85; officers 123–4; on a functional basis 63–

65; on a product basis 63; personal contacts in 125–6; regional 61–2
Computer Machinery Corporation 25–6
conflict: between company and nation 20, 77, 135, 148–56; between large and small companies 24; between local and home companies 119–20
consumers 93
corporation *see* multinational companies

DAF (Holland) 113
decentralization and centralization 55–72; of financial management 76, 82
devaluation 79–80; signs of its approach 84–5
distribution, marketing 95
Drucker, Peter 148
Duncan, M. W. 89–91

economic growth 19
economic nationalism 83
education, labour relations 105
Egypt, trade unions 106
employees 66, 136; effect of local culture on 104–6 *see also* labour relations
Esso, 'Tiger' campaign 97–8
European Economic Community 143–58; expanded market 32; regulations 163, 168–9
exchange reserves, drain on 151
expatriates 136–7
expropriation 162, 164
extractive industries 151, 162, 164

173

175